The International Dictionary of Accounting Acronyms

Thomas W. Morris

Glenlake Publishing Company, Ltd.
Chicago • London • New Delhi

Fitzroy Dearborn Publishers
Chicago and London

© 1998 The Glenlake Publishing Company, Ltd.

ISBN: 1-888998-47-4

Library Edition: Fitzroy Dearborn Publishers, Chicago and London
ISBN: 1-884964-56-7

Printed in the Unites States of America

GPCo
1261 West Glenlake
Chicago, IL 60660
glenlake@ix.netcom.com

Contents

About the Author

Thomas W. Morris has an extensive background in writing, research and communications. He has written and edited numerous publications for the Practice Development Institute, a subsidiary of Friedman, Eisenstein, Raemer and Schwarts (FERS).

Preface

The *International Dictionary of Accounting Acronyms* contains approximately 2,000 accounting and related acronyms in current usage from a variety of areas of practice. Subject areas include business and management, banking, finance, economics, investments, real estate and statistics.

This volume is not intended to be either authoritative or exhaustive. Nor does the inclusion of an acronym represent an expression of the author's or publisher's opinion as to any trademark or other rights in an acronym. Nor should the omission of an acronym be interpreted as an indication of that acronym's lack of recognition or usage in practice. The Dictionary should not be relied upon as having any bearing upon the validity or ownership of any trademark. The failure to indicate that an acronym is a trademark is not intended to represent that no trademark exists in the acronym and does not affect any legal rights in such acronym. A reference to an owner of an acronym or to an acronym as a trademark likewise should not be relied upon for legal authority. Errors brought to the attention of the publisher and verified satisfactorily will be corrected in future editions.

Effort has been made to exclude terms that are obsolete or of extremely limited current use, and terms of only local interest. Acronyms and their terms that are seldom or no longer used, but have been superseded by other terminology, are included because some discussions and documents may involve the older terminology, if only because those terms made strong impressions during their long years of use.

Acronyms concerning business and professional services relevant to the practice of accounting are included to anticipate terms that a user may encounter in range of situations where an individual may be expected to be familiar with the vernacular. Acronyms connected primarily with a particular area of professional practice, such as insurance, or banking, include a brief indicator at the beginning of the listing.

Acronyms with multiple meanings, all of them in current usage, will be listed in alphabetical order of their spelled-out meaning. It is generally expected that the user will be able to rely on the context of the discussion or documents to guide him or her to the correct area of business for an acronym. However, most acronyms still require a brief explanation of their meaning in addition to a spelled-out meaning. Therefore, a supplemental explanation has been given to aid the user in understanding the acronym and the term it represents. Otherwise, it is generally expected that the user will be able to again rely on the context of the discussion or relevant documents to guide him or her to the correct terminology. An acronym and its term can be presumed to be used within the United States unless stated otherwise.

A

AAA   **American Accounting Association**
The association that influences the development of Generally Accepted Accounting Principles through research of its professional membership.

AAII   **American Association of Individual Investors**
Chicago-based organization providing educational and networking opportunities and publications for the individual investor community. Publications and services include:

- The monthly *AAII Journal*
- A yearly tax planning guide
- A *Guide to Computerized Investing*. A directory listing accounting, financial, estate and tax planning software packages, among others.
- Nationwide seminars

AAII can be contacted at:
625 North Michigan Avenue, Suite 1900
Chicago, Illinois 60611
800-428-2244

AAPC   **Adjusted Average Per Capita Cost**
Business accounting and marketing term relating to adjustments made to average per capita costs to increase the accuracy of an analysis.

AAR   **Against All Risks**
Insurance term (applied elsewhere as well) to

identify condition of having identified risks connected with a planned insured or other venture.

AARS **Accrual Accounting and Reporting System**
Accounting term describing treatment of revenues when expected to be received and expenses when projected to be paid, as compared to Cash Accounting and Reporting System

AAS **Advanced Accounting System**
A general accounting term.

ABA **American Bankers Association**
A professional association offering programs, products and services for the banking community. National source of information and commentary on banking issues. The ABA is located at:

1120 Connectcut Ave., N.W.
Washington, D.C. 20036
(202) 663-5000, *fax* (202) 663-7543
www.aba.com

ABA **American Bar Association**
A professional association offering programs, products and services to the legal community. National source of information and commentary on legal issues. The ABA can be located at:

750 N. Lake Shore Drive
Chicago, IL 60611
(312) 988-5000

ABC **[ACCOUNTING METHOD]**
Inventory control method which categorizes by order of importance (*e.g.*, *A*s are higher-valued items, *B*s are lower-valued items and *C*s are items

with the lowest priority in terms of control and attention.

ABS   **Asset-Backed Securities**
Bonds or notes backed by loans or accounts receivable originated by banks, credit card companies or other providers of credit. Brokerage firms that reoffer them to the public underwrite the securities. Also called Pass-Through Securities.

ABS   **Automated Bond System**
Computerized system used by the New York Stock Exchange (NYSE) for recording bids and offers for inactively traded bonds until they are cancelled or executed.

AC   **Actual Cost**
Accounting term for exact amount as opposed to budgeted or expected amount in connection with a given expense.

ACES   **Advanced Computerized Execution System**
System run by the National Association of Securities Dealers (NASD), which owns and operates the National Association of Securities Dealers Automated Quotation System (NASDAQ).

ACRS   **Accelerated Cost Recovery System;**
                 Accelerated Capital Recovery System
Accounting and tax term concerning rules for depreciation of certain types of assets and property. The Economic Recovery Tax Act of 1981 made the cost of assets purchased after 1980 recoverable at an accelerated rate under the ACRS. *See also* ADR.

AcSEC   **Accounting Standards Executive Committee**
Committee of the American Institute of CPAs that
issues standards, regulations and guidelines for the
accounting profession.

Location:
AcSEC
AICPA, Inc.
Harborside Financial Center
201 Plaza III
Jersey City, NJ 07311-3881

ACU   **Asian Currency Unit**
A unit of a Singaporean bank that deals in foreign
currency deposits and loans.

ADB   **Adjusted Debit Balance**
Accounting and banking term to indicate revision
or adjustment made based on generally accepted
accounting principles (GAAP).

ADB   **Asian Development Bank**
A multilateral development financial institution
whose capital stock is owned by 56 member countries. The bank promotes the economic and social
progress of its development member countries in
the Pacific and Asian regions.

ADR   **Advance Determination Ruling**
Ruling issued by the Internal Revenue Service
(IRS).

ADR   **American Depository Receipt**
Investment instrument. Shares of foreign-based
corporations held in a U.S. bank. Shareholders are
entitled to dividends and capital gains. Americans

can buy shares of foreign-based companies in the U.S. instead of buying them in foreign countries.

ADR   **Asset Depreciation Range system**
Internal Revenue Service (IRS) system of guidelines that establish recommended ranges of depreciation to be applied to various classes of assets. *Also see* ACRS.

ADR   **Automatic Dividend Reinvestment**
An investment term for a program in which dividends are directly reinvested rather than paid out periodically to the investor. This allows investors to accumulate capital over the long term using "dollar cost averaging" (also referred to as constant dollar plan), which allows investors to invest a fixed amount of dollars at specified times. Thus, more shares are bought when the price is low and less shares are bought when the price is high.

ADS   **Annual Debt Service**
Accounting term for total annual amount paid by an investor in connection with a long-term loan (*e.g.*, mortgage).

AICPA   **American Institute of Certified Public Accountants**
The organization providing products, programs, and services to the accounting profession, self-regulatory oversight, and advisory and commentary to the business community at large on accounting and tax subjects. Their national headquarters:

AICPA, Inc.
1211 Avenue of the Americas
New York, NY 10036-8775
(212) 596-6200

AI   **Artificial Intelligence**
A computer software program that imitates human intelligence and learning from experience. AI performs complex strategies that assist in determining the best or worst way to accomplish a task or avoid problems.

AI programming languages include PROLOG, OPS5, POPLOG, ESIE, LISP and INTERLISP, a version of LISP.

AI applications include:
• Financial ratio analysis
• Management services
• Tax planning and preparation
• Planning and audit analysis
• Analyzing accounts receivable

Some AI programs include:
•*Taxadvisor* developed by R. Michaelson, University of Illinois. This program is used for estate planning.
• *Auditor* developed by C. Dungan, University of Illinois. This package is for examining bad debts.

AID   **Agency for International Development**
An organization providing and supporting funding and education from the U.S. to emerging nations.

AIS   **Accounting Information System**
Subsystem of Management Information System (*see* MIS) that comprises the activities involved in the preparation of financial information, and the information obtained from transactions for both internal and external reporting.

ALC   **Accelerated Loan Commitment**
Accounting and banking term for voluntary accel-
eration of payments by a borrower, generally to
decrease interest payments over the life of the
loan.

AMA   **American Management Association**
International organization providing a broad range
of programs, products and services to the business
community. Primary services include seminars,
books, audio/visual training tools, and the monthly magazine *Management Review*.

The U.S. headquarters is:
American Management Association
1601 Broadway
New York, NY 10019
800-262-9699
fax 518-891-3653

AMA   **Asset Management Account**
Investment term for a type of account that provides a variety or menu of investment and financial management and planning services with the
objective of centralizing several of an investor's
needs within one organization.

AMBAC   **American Municipal Bond Assurance
Corporation**
U.S. Government oversight organization involved
with municipal bond issues.

AMEX   **American Stock Exchange**
The U.S. stock exchange with the second biggest
volume of trading. Most securities traded on the
AMEX are small- to medium size companies and

include numerous oil and gas companies. In addition, the AMEX also trades the majority of foreign shares of any U.S. exchange. AMEX is located at:

86 Trinity Place
New York, NY 10006-1881
(212) 306-1000
www.amex.com

AMI   **Alternative Mortgage Instruments**
A generic descriptive term for mortgage financing other than conventional lenders.

AMPS   **Auction Market Preferred Stock**
Type of adjustable-rate preferred stock on which the dividend is determined every seven weeks in an auction process in which the price is gradually lowered until it meets a responsive bid from a corporate bidder.

AMS   **Agricultural Marketing Service**
A service of the United States government which assures purchasers of U.S. goods that they satisfy quality standards and contractual commitments.

AMT   **Alternative Minimum Tax**
Tax designed to ensure that high-income taxpayers do not pay too little in income taxes.

AMVI   **AMEX Market Value Index**
One of two major market indexes compiled by the American Stock Exchange. An unweighted index of AMEX stocks, computed as the sum of all of the plus net changes, minus net changes above or below previous closing prices. This sum is divided by the number of issues listed, and the result added to or subtracted from the previous close.

AOM   **Australian Options Market**
Sydney-based options market.

AON   **All or None**
In investment banking, an offering in which the
issuer has the right to cancel the entire issue if the
underwriting is not fully subscribed. In securities,
a buy or sell order marked to signify that no partial
transaction is to be executed.

A/P   **Accounts Payable**
Accounting term for bill payment systems and
processes.

APB   **Accounting Practice Bulletin**
One of a series of bulletins published by the
Financial Accounting Standards Board (FASB)
giving accountants guidance in applying Generally
Accepted Accounting Principles (GAAP) and
other rules and standards to new or unfamiliar
situations.

APR   **Annual Percentage Rate**
Lending term applied to credit or interest terms
stating the annualized percentage of interest on a
loan or a line of credit.

A/R   **Accounts Receivable**
Accounting term for systems and processes connected with payments owed to the organization.

ARM   **Adjustable Rate Mortgage**
Mortgage (generally residential) for which the
interest rate will be adjusted at certain pre-specified times during the life of the loan, based on prevailing indices at the time of adjustment, and

generally also carrying pre-specified limits on the percentage by which the interest rate can increase. Also called Variable Rate Mortgages and Flexible Rate Mortgages.

ARPS   **Adjustable Rate Preferred Stock**
Preferred stock whose dividend is adjusted based on changes in the Treasury bill rate or other money market rate, generally quarterly.

ARR   **Accounting Rate of Return**
Also called *simple rate of return*. Measures profitability from a conventional accounting point of view. ARR relates the required investment to the future annual net income. Rule of thumb: Select the project with the highest ARR. The formula is:

$$ARR = \frac{\text{Cash inflows} - \text{straight line depreciation}}{\text{Initial investment}}$$

Assume the following:

Initial investment	$20,000
Estimated life of investment	20 years
Cash inflows per year	$3,000
Straight line depreciation	$600

Then:

$$ARR = \frac{\$3,000 - \$600}{\$20,000} = 0.12\% \times 100 = 12\%$$

The average investment is usually assumed to be one half of the original investment. Thus, in this case, the investment amount is decreased each year by $600 and the ARR is computed by one half of the original cost. Thus, the ARR is doubled as follows:

ARR = $\dfrac{\$3,000 - \$600}{1/2\ \$20,000} = \dfrac{\$2,400}{\$10,000} = 0.24\% \times 100 = 24\%$

Disadvantage:
1. Does not take into account the time value of money
2. Uses accounting rather than cash flow information.

ARSC   **Accounting and Review Services Committee**
Committee under the American Institute of CPAs.

Location:
Accounting and Review Services Committee
AICPA, Inc.
Harborside Financial Center
201 Plaza III
Jersey City, NJ 07311-3881

ASB   **Auditing Standards Board**
The senior technical body of the American Institute of CPAs, designated to issue pronouncements on auditing matters.

Location:
Auditing Standards Board
AICPA, Inc.
Harborside Financial Center
201 Plaza III
Jersey City, NJ 07311-3881

ASCII   **American Standard Code for Information Interchange**
A standard code for conversion of characters to a binary number so that they are understandable by many microcomputers.

ASE   **Athens Stock Exchange**

ASP   **American Selling Price**
For customs purposes, the price used as a tax base for determining import duties.

ASPIRIN   **Australian Stock Price Riskless Indexed Notes**
Investment instrument.

ASX   **Australia Stock Exchange**

ATP   **Arbitrage Trading Program**
Investment banking program involving the simultaneous purchase and sale or exchange of securities or commodities in different (sometimes foreign) markets to profit from unequal prices. Also known as program trading.

B

BAL, BALCE   **Balance**

BAN   **Bond Anticipation Note**
Short-term debt investment instrument issued by a municipality or state. Issues are paid off with the returns from a bond issue.

B&F   **Business and Farm**
Banking descriptor for a particular type of property.

BBB   **Better Business Bureau**
Any of a group of local organizations in the U.S., supported by businessmen, functioning to receive and investigate customer complaints about area

businesses and make their findings available to the general public.

BC   **Bad Check or Bogus Check**
Banking term for a check uncollectable because either the account has insufficient funds or the check itself is fraudulent.

BCP   **Budget Change Proposal**
General business and accounting document for submitting a request for a revision to an existing budget or business plan.

BD   **Bank Draft**
Banking term for conventional paper check.

BE   **Bill of Exchange**
General business term for documentation involved in exchange (as opposed to purchase or sale) of goods or services.

B/E   **Break-Even Point**
General business term for number of units at which total direct and indirect costs connected with a program, product or service, are equal to revenue from sales of the same number of units, and beyond which sales begin to produce a profit.

BEA   **Break-Even Analysis**
General business term for spreadsheet or other calculation of a Break-Even Point. Formula:

Variable Costs + Fixed Expenses = Break-Even Sales

BF   **Bankruptcy Fee**
Australian finance term.

BF **Brought Forward**
Accounting term for amount carried from one time period to another.

BFC **Budget and Forecast Calendarization**
Accounting and general business term for allocating an annual budget across smaller time periods (quarterly or monthly).

BFCY **Beneficiary**
Insurance term for the designated person to receive the benefits of an insurance policy upon the demise of the insured.

BFY **Budget Fiscal Year**
Accounting and general business term for the dates on which an entity's financial year begins and ends (*e.g.*, Jan. 1 through Dec. 31, or July 1 through June 30).

BIC **Bank Investment Contract**
A bank-guaranteed interest in a portfolio providing a specified yield over a specified period of time.

BIN **Bank Identification Number**
U.S. banking term for number unique to each institution used for automated processing efficiencies.

BIP **Bureau of International Programs**
An agency of the U.S. Department of Commerce.

BKCY; BKY **Bankruptcy**
Banking and general business term for the condition of being adjudged financially insolvent.

BKG; BKPG   **Bookkeeping**
General business term for keeping account books.

BL; BILDG   **Bill of Lading**
General business term for documentation connected with freight shipping.

BLS   **Bureau of Labor Statistics**
U.S. Government agency that compiles and disseminates national statistics on labor and employment.

BMIR   **Below-Market Interest Rate**
Banking and general business term for lending terms below prevailing rates for similar loans.

B/O   **Back-Order; Back-Ordered**
General business term for goods out of stock and waiting to be replenished.

BOM   **Beginning of the Month**
Accounting and banking term used as indicator for commencement of accounting period or date on which a given financial transaction is scheduled.

BOMA   **Building Owners and Managers Association**
Washington, D.C.-based organization with subsidiaries throughout U.S., providing programs, products and services to individuals and organizations providing commercial and multi-unit residential property management services. Location:

1201 New York Ave., N.W.
Washington, D.C. 20005
(202) 408-2662, fax (202) 371-0181
www.boma.org

BOP **Balance of Payments**
Accounting and banking term for schedule on which remaining payments on a loan are due.

BOQ **Beginning of Quarter**
Accounting term for first date of a given fiscal quarter.

BOVESPA **Bolsa de Valores de Sao Paulo**
Largest of Brazil's nine stock exchanges.

BOY **Beginning of Year**
Accounting and general business term for the commencement of a new fiscal year.

BR **Bills Receivable**
Accounting term, similar to Accounts Receivable.

BRE **Business Reply Envelope**
General business term for postage-paid return envelopes, often used to increase response rate in direct-mail marketing campaigns and as a customer-service feature.

BS **Balance Sheet**
Accounting and general business term for a document that summarizes an organization's financial condition on a given date.

BS **Bill of Sale**
General business term for documentation for a purchase or sale of goods.

BSE **Bombay Stock Exchange**

BSE **Boston Stock Exchange**

BSE   **Brussels Stock Exchange**

BTR   **Bureau of Trade Regulation**
U.S. Department of Commerce organization.

BY   **Budget Year**
Australian business term for an organization's financial year.

C

CA   **Capital Account**
Banking and investment brokerage term for accounts that holds a significant proportion of an organization's or investor's wealth.

CA   **Capital Appreciation**
Banking term for return on investment of primary capital.

CA   **Chartered Accountant**
Certification of competency in accounting. Less rigorous than Certified Public Accountant.

CA   **Cost Account**
Accounting and general business term for account established for direct costs associated with production.

CA   **Cost Accountant**
Accounting term for personnel responsible for determining costs of items involved in production.

CA   **Credit Account**
Banking and accounting term for account

established in which credit can be drawn up to a specified amount.

CA   **Current Account**
Banking and Accounting term for account with ongoing activity.

CABNIS   **Consortia of American Businesses in the Newly Independent States**
U.S. Department of Commerce agency.

CACM   **Central American Common Market**

CACPAF   **Continental Association of CPA Firms**
London-based organization of CPA firms whose members practice and clients exist in both U.S. and Europe.

CAD   **Cash Against Documents**
Accounting term for comparison of current cash assets to long-term and other debt.

C&F   **Cost and Freight**
Exporter's quoted price and freight charges to the destination.

CAFR   **Comprehensive Annual Financial Report**
The annual report of a government. The report includes combined and individual balance sheets, as follows:

- All funds: Statement of revenues, expenditures and fund balance changes.
- General and special revenue funds: Statement of revenues, expenditures and fund balance changes.

• Proprietary funds: Statement of revenues, expenditures and retained earnings changes.

• Proprietary funds: Statement of changes in financial position.

CAPM   **Capital Asset Pricing Model**
Also called the *security market line (SML)*. Accounting and banking term for methodologies and guidelines used in setting a value on a capital asset. The CAPM relates the risk measured by beta to the level of expected or required rate of return on a security. Stated as follows:

$$r_j = r_f + b(r_m - r_f)$$

where: r_j is the expected (required) return on security j.
r_f is the risk-free security (*e.g.*, a T-bill)
r_m is the expected return on the market portfolio (*e.g.*, the S&P 500 or the DJIA)
b is an index of nondiversifiable, non controllable, systematic risk (*e.g.*, Beta).

Another option used to measure the cost of a stock using CAPM involves the following considerations:

1. The T-bill, considered the U.S. risk-free rate, *rf,* is estimated.
2. A stock's beta coefficient, *b,* an index of systematic (nondiversifiable market) risk is estimated.
3. A rate of return of a market portfolio (*e.g.*, S&P 500) is estimated.

4. The required rate of return on a firm's stock is estimated using the following formula:

$$k_e = r_f + b(r_m - r_f)$$

CAPS   **Convertible Adjustable Preferred Stock**
Preferred stock with an adjustable interest rate pegged to Treasury security rates and that can be exchanged, during the period after the announcement of each dividend rate for the next period, for common stock or cash with a market value equal to the par value of the stock.

CAPSR   **Cost Account Performance Status Report**
Accounting term for summary of accuracy in a prior time period of cost projections compared to reality.

CAS   **Contract Accounting Standard**
Accounting term for internally established standard against which a contract price is compared.

CATS   **Certificate of Accrual on Treasury Securities**
Investment term for document of accrued earnings on U.S. Treasury securities.

CAV   **Credit Account Voucher**
Banking term for document that indicates the amount of credit available in the stated account on a given date.

CB   **Cash Book**
Accounting term for summary of a cash account.

CB   **Credit Balance**
Accounting and banking term for amount of

credit available in a given account or to a given customer.

C/B   **Cost/Benefit**
General business term for quantitative and qualitative analysis of factors involved in a proposed venture.

CBA   **Certified Business Appraiser**
Certification offered by the Institute of Business Appraisers to those meeting established education and practice standards for appraising the value of a business.

CBA   **Chartered Bank Auditor**
Certification offered by the Bank Administration Institute.

CBA   **Cost-Benefit Analysis**
General business term for quantitative and qualitative analysis of factors involved in a proposed venture.

CBD   **Cash Before Delivery**
General business term specifying that payment is required before the vendor will make delivery.

CBD   **Central Business District**
Real estate term for densest and generally most desirable area of an urban area, in terms of both office and retail space.

CBD   **Commerce Business Daily**
Publication from the U.S. Department of Commerce, listing proposed government procurements, subcontracting leads and foreign business

opportunities. Government agencies are required to announce in the CBD all intended procurements of $25,000 or more, and potential suppliers have at least 30 days to respond.

CBE   **Certified Bank Examiner**
Professional certification by American Bankers Association.

CBO   **Collateralized Bond Obligation**
Investment bond backed by a pool of bonds rated BB or lower, generally packaged in high-risk, high-yield issues separated into three tiers of high-, medium- and low-quality collateral.

CBOT   **Chicago Board of Trade**
141 W. Jackson Blvd.
Chicago, IL 60604
(312) 697-7900

CBS   **Consolidated Balance Sheet**
Abbreviated summary of an organization's financial condition as of a given date.

CCA   **Current Cost Accounting**
Term for accounting of current direct costs associated with production.

CCH   **Commerce Clearing House**
U.S. publisher of authoritative texts on tax law, accounting and other business subjects.

CCP   **Cost Control Program**
General business term for an initiative undertaken by a business to institute changes directed at

reducing costs, generally without affecting production output or quality.

CD   **Certificate of Deposit**
Debt instrument issued by a bank that pays interest to the investor.

CDA   **Common Dollar Accounting; Constant
Dollar Accounting**
Australian accounting terms.

CE   **Capital Expenditure**
Accounting and general business term for
purchase of a tangible asset.

CE   **Cash Earnings**
Accounting and banking term for actual earnings
not reinvested and readily available for other uses.

CE   **Cost Effectiveness**
General business term for concept of soundness of
plans and practices based on direct and indirect
costs vs. income.

CEO   **Chief Executive Officer**
Officer of a firm or organization responsible for its
activities, sometimes used as an additional title by
the President, Chairman of the Board, Executive
Vice President or other officer.

CEP   **Capital Expenditure Proposal**
General business term for proposition that
involves a business making a major investment in,
e.g., equipment or real estate in order to enable a
new venture.

CF   **Carried Forward**
                    Accounting term for applying an expense from
                    one time period to another.

CFA   **Cash-Flow Accounting**
                    Accounting system that considers only cash and
                    does not deduct non-cash items such as
                    depreciation.

CFA   **Cash Flow Analysis**
                    Accounting term for financial analysis that consid-
                    ers only cash and does not consider non-cash items
                    such as depreciation.

CFA   **Chartered Financial Analyst**
                    Professional certification from the Association for
                    Investment Management and Research. The CFA
                    is awarded to those who pass a rigorous three-level
                    exam covering investment principles, asset valua-
                    tion and portfolio management, and have at least
                    three years of investment management experience.

CFAT   **Cash Flow After Taxes**
                    Accounting term for income less expenses (direct
                    and indirect) and taxes.

CFBT   **Cash Flow Before Taxes**
                    Accounting term for income less expenses (direct
                    and indirect).

CFC   **Cash Flow Component**
                    Accounting term for a type or category of income
                    or expense within a cash flow statement or
                    analysis.

CFD   **Corporate Finance Director**
                   Common job title for a corporate officer responsi-
                   ble for financial planning and recordkeeping.

CFE   **Certified Financial Examiner**
                   Professional certification from the Society of
                   Financial Examiners.

CFO   **Chief Financial Officer**
                   Common job title for a corporate officer responsi-
                   ble for handling funds, signing checks over a cer-
                   tain amount, financial planning and record-
                   keeping.

CFP   **Certified Financial Planner**
                   Professional designation offered by the Certified
                   Financial Planner Board of Standards.

CFRM   **Contract Financial Reporting Manual**
                   Documentation for a business' systems to main-
                   tain compliance with vendor and other contracts.

CFTC   **Commodities Futures Trading Commission**
                   Independent agency created by Congress to regu-
                   late the U.S. commodity futures and options mar-
                   kets, and to ensure market integrity and protect
                   market participants against manipulation, abusive
                   trade practices, and fraud.

CFY   **Company Fiscal Year**
                   Accounting and general business term referring to
                   the calendar by which a business' fiscal year
                   begins and ends.

CFY   **Current Fiscal Year**
                   Accounting and general business term designating

an event as occurring during the present financial accounting year.

CG **Capital Gain**
Accounting and tax term for the difference between the amount paid for an investment and the amount received for it when it is sold, when that amount is positive.

ChFC **Chartered Financial Consultant**
Financial planning professional designation awarded by the American College of the American Society of Chartered Life Underwriters. Requirements include successful completion of a ten-course program and three years' professional experience.

CHIPS **Clearinghouse Interbank Payment System**
A computerized clearing network systems for transfer of international dollar payments and settlement of interbank foreign exchange obligations.

CI **Cash Item**
Accounting term for income received or payment made in cash as opposed to securities or other obligations.

CIC **Chartered Investment Counselor**
Designation from the Investment Counsel Association of America (Washington D.C.), to those holding CFAs and currently working as investment counselors.

CIF **Corporate Income Fund**
Unit Investment Trust with a fixed portfolio of high-grade securities and other instruments, gener-

ally paying income to the investor on a monthly basis.

CIF   **Cost, Insurance and Freight**
General business term often used in financial records to group three common expense items that generally fluctuate equally based on numbers of units.

CIMC   **Certified Investment Management Consultant**
Designation from the Institute for Investment Management Consultants (based in Washington D.C., and Phoenix) to members who pass an examination and have at least three years of professional financial consulting experience.

CIMS   **Certified Investment Management Specialist**
Designation from the Institute for Investment Management Consultants (based in Washington D.C., and Phoenix) to associate members who pass an examination and meet financial services work experience requirements.

CIO   **Corporate Information Officer**
Common job title that generally encompasses internal and external (public) information management and distribution functions.

CIP   **Capital Investment Program**
General business term for long-term plan for investing capital to meet specific objectives.

CIPS   **Certified International Property Specialist**
Professional certification from the National Association of Realtors.

CL   **Capital Loss**

Accounting and tax term for the occurrence of an investment being sold for less than the amount originally paid for it, sometimes with favorable tax consequences.

CLN   **Construction Loan Note**

Note issued by a municipality to finance construction of multi-family housing projects, generally maturing in three years or less and repaid with the proceeds of a long-term bond issue.

CLU   **Chartered Life Underwriter**

Professional financial planning certification, most closely aligned with the life insurance industry.

CM   **Contribution Margin**

Marginal income. Reflects the difference between sales and the variable costs of the product/service. The amount available to cover fixed costs and make profits. For example:

Sales = $16,000
Variable costs = $8,000
Contribution Margin = $8,000 ($16,000 - $8,000)

CM (Variance)   **Contribution Margin Variance**

The difference between the actual contribution margin per unit and the budgeted contribution margin times the number of units sold. Thus:

- CM variance = (Actual CM per unit – Budgeted CM per unit) x Actual sales
- The greater the actual CM over the budgeted indicates a favorable condition.

CMA   **Competitive Market Analysis**
Real estate term for an analysis that uses information on generally at least three sales of comparable properties in the recent past as a tool to establish the fair market value, and therefore the listing price for a property before placing it on the market.

CME   **Chicago Mercantile Exchange**
Trades foreign currency futures, commodity futures, financial futures, and options. Location:
30 S. Wacker Drive
Chicago, IL 60606
(312) 930-1000

CMO   **Collateralized Mortgage Obligation**
Type of mortgage-backed bond that separates mortgage pools into two maturity classes called tranches: companion bonds, and planned amortization class bonds. CMOs generally give investors a higher level of security than other mortgage-backed securities.

CMV   **Current Market Value**
General business term for price at which willing buyers and sellers trade similar products or services in an open marketplace.

CNS   **Continuous Net Settlement**
Method of clearing and settling securities that eliminates multiple fails in the same securities, accomplished by using a clearinghouse and a depository to match transactions to securities available in the firm's position, resulting in one net receive or delivery position at the end of the trading day.

COA **Chart of Accounts**
Accounting term for list of accounts for all types of income and expense, used as a tool for internal processing and reporting.

COBRA **Congressional Omnibus Budget Reconciliation Act**
Federal legislation that gives employees the right to carry their group health insurance coverage for up to 18 months after leaving the employer, by paying the full premium. The advantage to the employee is that the full premium of the group policy is generally lower than the individual rate on comparable coverage.

COBY **Current Operating Budget Year**
Accounting and general business term, usually identical to Fiscal Year.

COD **Cash on Delivery**
General business term for arrangement by which a freight or other delivery person receives payment in full from a customer in cash or certified check when delivery is made from a vendor. In securities, the requirement that delivery of securities to an institutional investor be in exchange for assets of equal value, which generally means cash; also called Delivery Against Cost (DAC) and Delivery vs. Payment (DV).

CODA **Cash or Deferred Arrangement**
More commonly known as a 401(k) plan, an employee benefit plan in which employees can elect, as an alternative to receiving taxable compensation, to contribute part of their salary and

other compensation pretax to a qualified tax-deferred retirement plan.

COFI   **Cost-of-Funds Index**
Index based on what financial institutions are paying on money market accounts, passbooks, certificates of deposit and other liabilities, used by mortgage lenders to set rates on adjustable rate mortgages (*see* ARM). The COFI tends to move more slowly than other indexes for ARMs.

COLA   **Cost of Living Adjustment**
General business term generally applied to salary and other pay-rate increases based on current national or local cost-of-living statistics.

COLI   **Cost of Living Index**
U.S. Government statistic, generally referred to as Consumer Price Index.

COLTS   **Continuously Offered Longer-Term Securities**
Investment banking term for category of securities.

COO   **Chief Operating Officer**
Common job title for corporate officer responsible for day-to-day operations of the organization.

CPA   **Certified Public Accountant**
Person holding an official certificate as an accountant, having fulfilled all legal and licensing requirements at the state level and with the AICPA.

CPA/PFS

Certified Public Accountant/Personal Financial Specialist

Designation awarded by the American Institute of CPAs to CPAs who pass an exam and meet work experience requirements.

CPI

Consumer Price Index

Often called the *cost-of-living index*. U.S. Government statistic reflecting the changes in the cost of buying a fixed bundle of goods (in the categories of food and beverages; housing; apparel; transportation; medical care; entertainment; and other) for a typical American family, based on the costs of the same goods and services at the base period established in 1967.

CPM

Critical Path Method

Project-management technique that uses a single time estimate for each activity, the primary objective being to identify the critical path for a project. *See also* PERT.

CRAT

Charitable Remainder Annuity Trust

A tax-exempt entity created as an estate-planning tool that pays a fixed and specified annuity amount to one or more person living at the inception of the arrangement, either for life or for a term of years not to exceed twenty.

CRT

Charitable Remainder Trust

Accounting term for a planned giving vehicle in which an asset is placed in trust to benefit a charitable organization and the donor receives tax benefits.

CRUT   **Charitable Remainder Unit Trust**
A tax-exempt entity that pays a fixed, specified percentage of the trust property valued annually to one or more person living at the inception of the arrangement, either for life or for a term of years not to exceed twenty.

CRV   **Certificate of Reasonable Value**
Document from an appraiser or other valuation expert, describing an asset or piece of property and attesting to its value based on its current condition at a specific point in time.

C/S   **Cost of Sale**
Accounting and general business term for expenses in connection with the sale of an asset.

CSP   **Classification Settlement Program**
IRS program in which tax examiners can offer settlements to businesses that have incorrectly classified workers (*e.g.*, as independent contractors as opposed to full-time or part-time employees). The program is voluntary and businesses that decline an offered settlement retain their right to appeal.

CSVLI   **Cash Surrender Value of Life Insurance**
Insurance term for the contract specified cash value of a life insurance policy if that option is exercised by the insured. The insurance premium consists of both expense and cash surrender value. *Example*: A premium of $12,000 is paid that increases the cash surrender value by $8,000. The appropriate entry is:

Life Insurance Expense	4,000
Cash Surrender Value of Life Insurance	8,000
Cash	12,000

CTA   **Cumulative Translation Adjustment Account**
Account entry in a translated balance sheet where
gains and/or losses from currency translation have
accumulated over a period of years.

CVP   **Cost Volume Profit**
Useful for analyses by managers. Deals with how
profit and costs change with a change in volume.
Managers look at the relationships of costs, sales
and net income to better cope with planning decisions and determine break-even sales (*i.e.*, the
level of sales where total costs equal total
revenue).

A difference is made between variable and
fixed costs in order to perform accurate CVP
analysis. The following concepts are considered:

CM (Contribution Margin) which is the excess
of sales (S) over variable costs (VC) of a product.
That is, it is the money available to cover fixed
costs (FC) and produce profits. Thus,
CM = S – VC.

Unit CM, the excess of unit selling price (p)
over the unit variable cost (v). Represented as
CM = p – v.

CM Ratio is the contribution margin as a percentage of sales. That is,

$$\text{CM ratio} = \frac{CM}{S} = \frac{S - VC}{S} = 1 - \frac{VC}{S}$$

CVP analysis determines what sales volume is
needed to break even, volume needed to earn a
desired profit, the profit expected on a given sales
volume, how selling price, variable costs, fixed
costs and output affect profit, and how changing
the mix of products sold will affect break-even and
income and profit potential.

CWO   **Cash with Order**
Merchandise is paid for when purchased rather than when delivered.

D

DA   **Deposit Account**
Accounting and banking term for an account that was established solely to receive deposited funds, from which funds are transferred to other accounts as necessary.

DA   **Discretionary Account**
Accounting and general business term for account from which funds can be drawn by authorized persons for a broad range of business-related expenses.

DBA   **Doing Business As**
Banking and general business term referring to the name of a business enterprise used in place of the owner's actual name and recorded with the county in which the business is located.

DBMS   **Data Base Management System**
Group of computer software packages that integrates data in one place for sharing by all systems on a network, allowing cross-referencing of data among files to eliminate repetition.

DCF   **Discounted Cash Flow**
Accounting and investment analysis concept that uses the future projected value of an investment

discounted to its present-day value as a means of evaluating the relative merits of the investment.

DDB   **Double-Declining Balance Depreciation Method**
Accounting and tax term for using an accelerated depreciation of certain types of assets in financial reporting and tax planning.

DE   **Double Entry**
Accounting term for simultaneous entry of one transaction in two sets of records.

DENK   **Dual-Employed, No Kids**
Term for a category of taxpayers with common issues: married couples both of whom work, without children. (similar to DINK; *Also see* DEWK)

DEWK   **Dual-Employed, With Kids**
Term for a category of taxpayers with common issues: married couples both of whom work, with children. (*Also see* DENK, INK)

DIF   **Data Interchange Format (File)**
Computer system feature that allows for the transfer of files between systems and between different programs in the same system, such as between a spreadsheet program and a word-processing program.

DINK   **Double Income, No Kids**
Term similar to DENK; *Also see* DEWK.

DISC   **Domestic International Sales Corporation**
Domestic corporations created by the Revenue Act

of 1971 to encourage exports and, thus, improve the balance of trade.

DJIA   **Dow Jones Industrial Average**
Most widely followed stock market average, a benchmark stock average of 30 blue chip industrial stocks selected for total market value and broad public ownership and believed to reflect overall market activity, established in 1884.

DN   **Debit Note**
Written promise to pay a specified amount to a named entity on demand or on a specified date.

DOA   **Documents of Acceptance**
An international trade procedure used for payment of goods.

D/P   **Deferred Payment**
Accounting and general business term for arrangement in which payment for goods or services is not required at the time the goods or services are delivered.

DPI   **Disposable Personal Income**
Tax accounting and financial planning term for personal income not needed for basic necessities and therefore available for discretionary expenditures, such as travel, entertainment, etc.

DRIP   **Dividend Reinvestment Plan**
Investment vehicle (such as stock) in which dividends are automatically used to purchase additional shares rather than paid out to the investor.

DSS   **Decision Support System**
Computer software that supports decision-making
processes, including planning and forecasting, risk
and trend analysis and what-if analyses.

DT   **Debits Tax**
Australian taxation term.

DTB   **Deutsche Terminborse**
Fully computerized exchange in Germany

DTC   **Depository Trust Company**
Member of the Federal Reserve System owned by
brokerage houses and the New York Stock
Exchange, a centralized securities repository
where stock and bond certificates are exchanged.

DUS   **Dollar Unit Sampling**
Auditing test that uses a probability proportionate
to size sampling of audit units with a high preci-
sion level of possible error based on dollar mis-
takes found in a random sample, combined with an
attribute resulting from a probability determination. DUS is generally used only when a low rate
of sampling errors is expected.

DVA   **Discovery Value Accounting**
Australian accounting method.

E

EAN   **Expenditure Account Number**
Accounting term for general account used to paying day-to-day expenses of a business.

EBB **Economic Bulletin Board**
A computer-based electronic bulletin board that provides leads and up-to-date statistical releases from the Bureau of Census, the Bureau of Economic Analysis, the Bureau of Labor Statistics, the Federal Reserve Board and other federal agencies. Connecting to the EBB can be done with a personal computer and modem by dialing: 202-482-3870.

EBIT **Earnings before Interest and Taxes**
Accounting term used to clarify whether the accounting and reporting of an investment's earnings reflect interest and tax expenses.

EBITA **Earnings before Interest, Taxes, Depreciation and Amortization**
Accounting term used to clarify whether the accounting and report of an investment's earnings reflect interest, taxes, etc.

EC **European Community**
General business and economics term for specific group of European nations.

ECU **European Currency Unit**
Composite currency created to function as a reserve currency numeraire. Consists of fixed amounts of the currencies of the members of the European Economic Community (EEC).

EDR **European Depository Receipt**
A means for trading of foreign investments by Americans in the securities of foreign countries.

EE   **Equity Earnings**
Accounting and financial management term for earnings on investment equity.

EEC   **European Economic Community**
General business and economics term for specific group of European nations.

EERPF   **Eastern European Real Property Foundation**
U.S. Government agency developed to educate Eastern European governments and businessmen about various aspects of the real estate industry and its practices in the U.S.

EFT   **Electronic Funds Transfer**
Accounting and banking term for mechanism for automatic and paperless transfers of funds between accounts or organizations.

EFTPS   **Electronic Federal Tax Payment System**
IRS system available to all taxpayers for filing tax returns and making tax payments electronically.

EIOP   **End of Initial Operating Period**
Accounting and general business term for specific date established for end of a new enterprise's start-up phase.

EMP   **End of Month Payment**
Accounting and banking term to indicate scheduled payment to/from a certain account.

EMR   **Experience Modification Rate**
Accounting and insurance term for the ratio of a company's losses to expected losses based on the industry and classification averages over a

three-year period. used in calculating workers' compensation insurance premiums.

$$\frac{\text{Actual Losses}}{\text{Expected Losses}} = \text{EMR}$$

EMS   **European Monetary System**
A small international monetary fund system formed in 1979 by 12 European countries. Under the system, member countries agreed to maintain their exchange rates within an established range about a fixed central rate in relation to one another.

EOM   **End of the Month**
A credit designation that usually means payment is due at the end of the current month the purchase was made.

EOQ   **Economic Order Quantity**
Model that determines the order size that minimizes the sum of carrying costs and order costs, computed as the square root of:

$$\frac{2(\text{Annual demand})(\text{Ordering cost})}{\text{Carrying cost per unit}}$$

EOY   **End of Year**
Accounting term used in financial reporting to indicate financial information (actual or anticipated) for the end of the organization's fiscal year.

EPR   **Earnings Price Ratio (more commonly Price-Earnings Ratio)**
General financial term for ratio of a share's market price to the company's earnings per share.

EPS   **Earnings Per Share**
Financial ratio for the amount of net income attributable to each share of common stock. This is the most widely watched ratio. EPS measures corporate operating performance and expected future dividends. The formula is:

$$EPS = \frac{\text{Net Income} - \text{Preferred Dividends}}{\text{Common Shares Outstanding}}$$

A decrease in EPS over the year should alert investor.

ER   **Expense Report**
General term for forms and other paperwork connected with accounting and reimbursement to individuals for certain business expenses (such as business travel and entertainment).

ERISA   **Employee Retirement Income Security Act of 1974**
Federal legislation that enacted broad changes in retirement benefits for corporate employees.

ERTA   **Economic Recovery Tax Act of 1981**
Federal legislation that enacted broad changes to in general reduce income tax liabilities for U.S. taxpayers.

ESOP   **Employee Stock Ownership Plan**
Mechanism for converting all or part of the private ownership in a company into shares that are given to employees as bonuses, or sold to employees under certain terms.

EV   **Economic Value**
Accounting and banking term for the monetary

value of an asset, excluding intangible factors and possible future events that may affect the valuation.

F

FA   **Fixed Asset**

Accounting term for an asset whose value is generally not subject to fluctuations caused by market forces.

FAF   **Fly Away Free**

FAQ   **Frequently Asked Questions**

FAS   **Financial Accounting Standard**

Declaration by the Financial Accounting Standards Board regarding the correct meaning and application of a particular financial accounting rule.

FASAB   **Federal Accounting Standards Advisory Board**

Government agency located at:

Federal Accounting Standards Advisory Board
441 G Street, N.W.
Washington, D.C. 20548

FASB   **Financial Accounting Standards Board**

Recognized authoritative body for establishing and maintaining accounting principles in the U.S.

Location:
FASB
401 Merritt 7
P.O. Box 5116
Norwalk, CT 06856-5116

FBT   **Fringe Benefits Tax**
Any federal income tax paid on an employee benefit received outside of salary but classified by the IRS as taxable income to the employee.

FC   **Full Charge**
Accounting and general business term indicating that a cost will be charged and paid at 100% and not discounted.

FCIA   **Foreign Credit Insurance Association**
A private U.S. insurance carrier that insures exporters.

FDI   **Foreign Direct Investment**
Investments that involve ownership of a company in a foreign country.

FDIC   **Federal Deposit Insurance Corporation**
Insurance company for U.S. banks and their depositors.

FET   **Federal Estate Tax**
Area of the federal tax code concerned with taxpayers' estates and those parts that are transferred to others or passed on to heirs.

FET   **Federal Excise Tax**
Taxes on certain consumer items, such as alcohol, tobacco, gasoline, firearms and airline tickets.

FFB   **Federal Financing Bank**
                   U.S. government-owned bank that consolidates
                   financing activities of various government agen-
                   cies to reduce borrowing costs.

FGL   **Financial General Ledger**
                   Accounting term interchangeable with General
                   Ledger.

FGT   **Federal Gift Tax**
                   Area of the federal tax code concerned with tax-
                   payers' gifts to others and the tax benefits and
                   liabilities thereby created.

FHA   **Federal Housing Administration**
                   U.S. Government agency that insures lenders
                   against loss on residential mortgages.

FHFB   **Federal Housing Finance Board**
                   U.S. Government agency that oversees the Federal
                   Home Loan Bank system, which replaced the
                   Federal Home Loan Bank Board.

FHLMC   **Federal Home Loan Mortgage Corporation**
                   Commonly called Freddie Mac, also refers to
                   mortgage-backed securities packaged, guaranteed
                   and sold by the organization.

FIA   **Fixed Income Account**
                   Accounting and banking term for account of a
                   fixed-income investment.

FIC   **Financial Inventory Control**
                   Accounting term for practices connected with
                   monitoring inventory, ordering levels, and
                   inventory costs.

FICA   **Federal Insurance Contributions Act, commonly known as Social Security**
Federal legislation that provides retirement income and health benefits to the elderly, disabled and other qualifying individuals and families.

FICR   **Financial Inventory Control Report**
Accounting and business management term for periodic reporting of inventory levels and costs used to optimize use of financial resources.

FICS   **Financial Information Control System**
Accounting and business management term for systems governing flow, management and access to financial information.

FICS   **Forecasting and Inventory Control System**
Accounting and business management term for system that anticipates and plans for inventory fluctuations.

FIFO   **First In, First Out**
Accounting term for method of valuing inventory and calculating taxable profit. When inventory is sold, the cost of what was bought first is charged against what was sold before later purchases are charged. (*Also see* FISH, LIFO)

FIR   **Financial Inventory Report**
Accounting and business management term for periodic inventory report.

FIRREA   **Financial Institutions Reform, Recovery and Enforcement Act**
Federal tax legislation enacted in 1989 to resolve the crisis in the savings and loan industry.

FIS   **Fiscal Information System**
                        Accounting and business management term for
                        general financial management information
                        systems.

FISH   **First In, Still Here**
                        Facetious accounting term for unsold, aging
                        inventory. *Also see* FIFO, FIST, LIFO.

FIST   **First In, Still There**
                        Facetious inventory accounting term. *Also see*
                        FIFO, FISH, LIFO

FIT   **Federal Income Tax**
                        Broad area of the federal tax code concerned with
                        tax obligations owed on all types of income
                        (earned income, capital gains, etc.)

FITW   **Federal Income Tax Withholding**
                        Accounting and tax term for systems of withhold-
                        ing Federal Income Taxes from payments to work-
                        ers for payment directly to the U.S. Government.

FLR   **Fixed Loan Rate**
                        Accounting and banking term for fixed lending
                        rate as opposed to variable rate over the life of a
                        loan.

FMR   **Fair Market Rent**
                        Business and real estate term for the rental rate
                        based on comparisons to rental rates to similar
                        properties in similar locations at same period of
                        time.

FMRR   **Financial Management Rate of Return**
                        Accounting and real estate investment term for

analysis that measures return on investment during length of ownership, refined to remove certain distortions during periods of negative cash flow. *Also see* IRR.

FNMA   **Federal National Mortgage Association**
U.S. mortgage agency, commonly called Fannie Mae.

FOB   **Free On Board**
Accounting and business management term for delivery charges for merchandise brought to a certain named location.

FOK   **Fill or Kill**
In securities brokerage, signifies a buy or sell order that will be cancelled if a complete transaction is not executed.

FOMC   **Federal Open-Market Committee**
Division of the Federal Reserve Bank, responsible for setting interest rates and credit policies for the Federal Reserve System. Economists and market analysts watch the Committee's decisions closely as a means of predicting action by the Fed to stimulate the economy by tightening or loosening credit.

FP   **Fully Paid**
Accounting and bookkeeping term for an invoice or loan paid in full.

FRB   **Federal Reserve Board**
Governing board of the Federal Reserve System, establishing Federal Reserve System policies on reserve requirements and other bank regulations,

setting the discount rate, controlling the availability of credit in the country, and regulating the purchase of securities on margin.

FREIT   **Finite Life Real Estate Investment Trust**
A Real Estate Investment Trust (*see* REIT) that is established with the goal of selling its holdings within a specified period of time to realize capital gains.

FSC   **Foreign Sales Corporation**
Established by the Tax Reform Act of 1984. The FSC is a foreign corporation that exports for a United States firm. The firm may show its profits in the FSC and avoid U.S. taxation on a percentage of the earnings until they are remitted to the parent U.S. firm.

FSLIC   **Federal Savings and Loan Insurance Corporation**
Insurance company for savings and loan institutions and their depositors.

FTC   **Federal Trade Commission**
U.S. Government agency charged with investigating and enjoining illegal practices in interstate trade.

FTI   **Federal Tax Included**
Accounting term to indicate that federal taxes are included in a certain number.

FTI   **Foreign Traders Index**
The index, compiled by the United States and Foreign Commercial Service, covers information about foreign entities, including addresses, contact

persons, revenue, company size, and product or services offered.

FTO   **Foreign Trade Organization**
A government trading company run by a communist country.

FTT   **Federal Transfer Tax**
Large area of the federal tax code that comprises three tax regimes: federal estate tax (FET); federal gift tax (FGT); and the generation-skipping tax (GST).

FUTA   **Federal Unemployment Tax Act**
Federal and state legislation that requires employers to contribute to a fund that pays unemployment insurance benefits for employees.

FV   **Face Value**
Australian accounting and banking term for the value of a bond, note or security as given on the certificate or instrument.

FV   **Future Value**
Accounting and financial analysis term for projected value of an investment at a specified point in time.

FVO   **For Valuation Only**
(related to FYI—For Your Information)

FX   **Foreign Exchange**
An instrument employed in making payments between countries, whether paper or electronic.

FY   **Fiscal Year**
                 Accounting term for a business entity's financial
                 reporting year (*e.g.*, January 1 through December
                 31, or July 1 through June 30)

FYDS   **Fiscal Year Data Summary**
                 Accounting term for a preliminary or interim
                 financial report.

FYE   **Fiscal Year Ending**
                 Accounting abbreviation, such as "FYE June 30,
                 1999."

FYM   **Fiscal Year Month**
                 Accounting term used when the numbers 1
                 through 12 rather than months' names are used in
                 financial reporting and recordkeeping. such as
                 "FYM1" in place of January.

FYO   **Fiscal Year Option**
                 Accounting term for an entity's opportunity to
                 change its financial reporting year, for instance
                 from January 1 through December 31, to July 1
                 through June 30, to accommodate certain season-
                 alities in business cycles.

G

GAAP   **Generally Accepted Accounting Principles**
                 Conventions, rules, guidelines and detailed proce-
                 dures that define accepted accounting practice, set
                 forth by the Financial Accounting Standards
                 Board.

GAAS   **Generally Accepted Auditing Standards**
Accounting term for body of knowledge for proper conducting accounting audits, promulgated by the AICPA and interpretations of which are issued in the form of Statements on Auditing Standards (SAS). The ten fundamental standards are grouped as follows: general standards, standards of fieldwork, and reporting standards.

GAI   **General Accounting Instructions**
Accounting term for internal documents codifying day-to-day and other accounting and financial management and reporting practices and requirements.

GAS   **General Accounting Service**
British agency similar to U.S. Financial Accounting Standards Board.

GASB   **Governmental Accounting Standards Board**
U.S. Government agency establishing accounting standards for both government and business.

Location:
GASB
401 Merritt 7
P.O. Box 5116
Norwalk, CT 06856-5166

GATR   **Gross Average Tax Rate**
Australian tax term.

GATT   **General Agreement on Tariffs and Trade**
International trade agreement initiated by the United Nations that eliminates trade barriers

between nations. GATT has four basic long-term objectives:

1. reduction of tariffs by negotiation
2. elimination of import quotas
3. nondiscrimination in trade through adherence to unconditional most-favored nation treatment
4. resolution of differences through arbitration and consultation

GCM   **General Counsel Memoranda**
Background documents that the IRS uses to support a ruling, useful to accountants as research tools to interpret the Internal Revenue Code (IRC).

GD   **Gross Debt**
Accounting business term for total loans outstanding to creditors.

GDP   **Gross Domestic Product**
Interchangeable with Gross National Product (GNP), which is more often used.

GE   **Gross Earnings**
Accounting term for an entity's total earnings (e.g., both dividends and interest) in a given earnings period.

GEM   **Growing Equity Mortgage or Growth Equity Mortgage**
Fixed-rate home loan with a fixed interest rate for the life of the loan, but annual payment increases as set by the loan agreement, with the increases applied directly to the principal. This type of loan is often attractive to first-time homebuyers and others who cannot afford a large down payment or

higher interest payments during the early years of the loan, but whose earning power can be expected to increase over the life of the loan.

GI   **Gross Income**
Term for total income from a business or property.

GIC   **Guaranteed Investment Contract**
Contract between an insurance company and a corporation's profit sharing or pension plan that guarantees a specific rate of return on invested capital over the life of the contract.

GJ   **General Journal**
Accounting term for day-to-day bookkeeping records of receipts and disbursements.

GL   **General Ledger**
Accounting term for bookkeeping of all financial records.

GLA   **General Ledger Account**
Accounting and bookkeeping term for account active within an entity's general ledger system.

GLAC   **General Ledger Account Code**
Accounting term for an account used at all levels of the general ledger system for consistency.

GLAPPAR   **General Ledger, Accounts Payable, and Accounts Receivable**
Accounting term for this group of accounting and bookkeeping functions.

GLIC   **General Ledger Identification Code**
Accounting term for coding of items for consistency.

GLPA   **General Price Level Accounting**
Australian term.

GLSA   **General Ledger Subsidiary Account**
Accounting term for secondary level of general ledger bookkeeping.

GMV   **Guaranteed Minimum Value**
General business and marketing term for a value below that a commodity is guaranteed by the vendor not to fall.

GNMA   **Government National Mortgage Association**
Commonly called Ginnie Mae, a government-owned corporation that primarily issues securities that pass through all payments of interest and principal received on a pool of federally insured mortgage loans. GNMA guarantees that all payments of principal and interest will be made on the mortgages on a timely basis.

GNP   **Gross National Product**
The monetary value of all the goods and services, minus depreciation and consumption, produced in a country.

GPM   **Graduated Payment Mortgage**
Real estate lending instrument in which payments gradually increase over a set period and the interest rate is adjusted periodically according to a specified economic index.

GPP　　　　**General Purchasing Power**
Economics term for aggregate potential for consumption among a specific demographic population.

GRAT　　　　**Grantor Retained Annuity Trust**
An estate-planning mechanism in which an asset is placed in a trust for a certain period of time and the grantor receives income from an annuity. If the donor dies before the term expires, then the entire value of the transferred property, valued at the donor's death, is taxed as part of the donor's gross estate for federal estate tax (FET) purposes. However, if the donor survives the term, the entire property is passed to the donee at only a fraction of the federal gift tax (FGT) value that would otherwise attend such passing.

GRIT　　　　**Grantor Retained Income Trust**
Financial planning vehicle for passing increased wealth to heirs by reducing estate and inheritance taxes, and protecting the grantor's primary residence from the claims of creditors.

GRM　　　　**Gross Rent Multiplier**
Real estate term for a "rule-of-thumb" measure of value.

GSI　　　　**Gross Scheduled Income**
Real estate income as derived by multiplying monthly rent per current lease by 12 months.

GST　　　　**Generation-Skipping Tax**
Large area of the federal tax code concerned with gifts and exemptions available to all taxpayers against transfers during life or at death, and the

estate-planning mechanisms that can be used to create long-term trusts that protect assets from over-taxation.

GTC   **Good Till Cancelled**
A customer's order to a broker to buy or sell securities at a specified price, which is to remain in effect until it is either executed, or cancelled by the customer.

GULP   **Group Universal Life Policy**
Life insurance policy offered to employees and, sometimes, their family members, on a group basis, therefore less expensively than individuals could obtain personally.

H

HA   **House Account**
Financial management. An account handled at the main office of a brokerage firm or managed by an executive of the firm, as distinguished from an account managed by a salesperson.

HC   **Hard Copy**
Business management term for a physical paper document as opposed to an electronic document.

HC   **Holding Company**
Business management term for a corporation that owns enough voting stock in another corporation to influence its board of directors and therefore to control its policies and management.

HCB   **Hungarian Credit Bank**

HEL   **Home Equity Loan**
Loan that uses the borrower's primary residence
and equity as collateral, generally used to finance
home improvements, generally with financing
terms more attractive than the borrower would be
able to obtain with a conventional loan.

HICB   **Hong Kong Industrial and Commercial Bank**

HIC   **Highly Indebted Country**
International finance term for nations carrying
large amounts of indebtedness to other nations.

HK$ **Hong Kong Dollar**

HKCE   **Hong Kong Commodities Exchange**

HKFE   **Hong Kong Futures Exchange**

HLT   **Highly Leveraged Transaction**
Loan, usually by a bank to a company whose capital structure includes debt in addition to equity .

HMO   **Health Maintenance Organization**
Relatively recent development in health-care plans
for employees of businesses and others in which
individuals' needs are served by certain providers
as opposed to individually chosen physicians, etc.,
to control costs and set and maintain certain standards of care.

HP   **Half Pay**
Business management term for a 50% rate

reduction in a worker's fee for a given period for a specific reason.

HP   **Half Price**
Business management for a 50% price discount on a product or service.

HPR   **Holding Period Return, or annual rate of return**
HPR for mutual funds is calculated by incorporating dividends, capital gains and price appreciation being ending NAV – beginning NAV. The formula is:

$$HPR = \frac{[Dividend + Capital\ gain\ distribution + (Ending\ NAV - Beginning\ NAV)]}{Beginning\ NAV}$$

HRA   **Human Resource Accounting**
Specialized field within accounting dealing with human resources, payroll and employee benefits, taxes and other issues, generally viewing employees as valuable assets and striving to enhance the positive relationship between a business' success and the quality of its employees. Primary objectives include quantifying the business' human resources for use in decision-making, and evaluating and managing costs of turnover.

HUD   **U.S. Department of Housing and Urban Development**
U.S. Government agency responsible for stimulating and guiding the housing development industry.

I

IA	**Inactive Account** Banking and brokerage term for an account not generally used continually in a productive way.
IAAO	**International Association of Assessing Officers** Chicago, Ill.-based trade organization of individuals offering a range of valuation and assessment services to business and industry.
IABK	**International Association of Book-Keepers** British-based trade organization.
IAFP	**International Association for Financial Planning** Atlanta, Ga.-based trade organization.
IAHA	**International Association of Hospitality Accountants** Washington, D.C.-based organization.
IAP	**Insurance Accounting Principles** Accounting term for body of principles specific to insurance issues.
IAPC	**International Auditing Practices Committee** A committee of the International Federation of Accountants (IFA) that has the responsibility and authority to issue exposure drafts and guidelines on Generally Accepted Auditing Standards. Its primary objective is the "development and enhancement of a coordinated worldwide accountancy profession with harmonized standards."

IAR   **Inventory Adjustment Rate**
                 Accounting term for rate applied to inventory
                 under certain conditions to correct or clarify
                 probable errors.

IARFP   **International Association of Registered
                 Financial Planners**
                 New Jersey-based trade organization.

IASC   **International Accounting Standards
                 Committee**
                 International self-regulatory organization for the
                 accounting industry.

                 Location:
                 International Accounting Standards Committee
                 167 Fleet Street
                 London EC4A 2Es England

IAU   **International Accounting Unit**
                 The unit of measure used in NATO projects which
                 is based on the exchange rates of the member
                 nations and is reevaluated every six months.

IBF   **International Banking Facility**
                 A banking operation within United States bank
                 that allows it to accept eurocurrency deposits from
                 foreign residents without the need for
                 domestic reserve requirements, interest rates ceil-
                 ings, or deposit insurance premiums.

IBI   **Islamic Bank International**

IBRD   **International Bank for Reconstruction and
                 Development**
                 Also known as the World Bank, the organization

that provides financing for commercial and infrastructure projects, mostly in developing nations.

IC   **Incremental Cost**
Accounting term for a cost factor that increases in proportion to one or more variables.

IC   **Independent Contractor**
Business management term for an individual providing services or works for hire for a fee to a company as opposed to being an employee, in a relationship governed by IRS regulations and guidelines.

IC   **Investment Tax Credit**
Tax accounting term for a reduction in income tax liability granted by the U.S. Government to firms making new investments in certain asset categories, such as equipment.

ICA   **International Congress of Accountants**
A worldwide organization of the major professional organizations of accountants whose main objective is to deal with problems relating to the diversity of accounting principles and practices from differing countries

ICC   **Interstate Commerce Commission**
U.S. Government agency created to ensure that the public receives fair and reasonable rates and services from carriers and transportation service firms involved in interstate commerce.

IC&C   **Invoice Cost and Charges**
Accounting and bookkeeping term for the total amount of an itemized bill for goods or services as

prepared by the seller, including the goods and services, and applicable taxes, delivery and other charges.

ICCA **Institut Canadien de Comptables Agrees**
Canadian Institute of Chartered Accountants.

ICEM **Incremental Cost Effectiveness Model**
Business management term for analytical framework for determining cost effectiveness of various possible outcomes given certain variables.

ICFP **Institute of Certified Financial Planners**
Denver, Colo.-based trade organization.

ICM **Inventory Control Management or Inventory Control Manager**
Business management term for the function or job title associated with managing and valuing supplies, finished goods, etc., of a business.

ICP **Inventory Control Point**
Accounting and business management term for a predetermined inventory level that triggers a certain event (*e.g.*, reordering) when reached.

ICR **Inventory Change Report**
Accounting and business management term for documentation completed to reflect an adjustment to inventory reporting, either as a correction or to record goods received, etc.

ICS **Issued Capital Stock**
Brokerage term for stock sold by a corporation or entity at a particular time.

ID   **Interest Deductible**
Tax accounting term for loan interest that is
deductible against corporate or individual income
tax.

ID   **Issue Date**
Brokerage term for date on which stock or securities were available for purchase.

IDB   **Industrial Development Bond**
Type of municipal revenue bond issued to finance
fixed assets that are then leased to private firms,
whose payments amortize the debt.

IDR   **Industrial Development Revenue Bond**
Interchangeable with Industrial Development
Bond (IDB).

IDR   **Invoice Discrepancy Report**
Accounting and business management term for a
periodic report summarizing variances between
departments or functions in terms of amount
invoiced and amount received.

IET   **Interest Equalization Tax**
Tax of 15% on interest received by foreign
borrowers in U.S. capital markets, imposed in
1963 and discontinued in 1974.

IF   **Insufficient Funds**
Accounting and banking term applied to a bank
draft written on an account that lacks adequate
funds to pay the amount of the draft.

IFAC   **International Federation of Accountants**
Professional organization located at:

International Federation of Accountants
535 Fifth Ave, 26th floor
New York, NY 10017

ILC, ILOC   **Irrevocable Letter of Credit**
Instrument or document issued by a bank guaranteeing the payment of a customer's drafts up to a
stated amount for a specified period and which
cannot be canceled.

ILCCTC   **International Liaison Committee on Co-
Operative Thrift and Credit**
Paris, France-based international finance
organization.

ILO   **International Labor Office**
An affiliate of the United Nations composed of
unions, employers, and governments dealing with
trade union rights, employment terms and conditions, and the protection of the right to work and
organize and bargain collectively.

I/M   **Inventory Management**
Business management term for the functions
involved with managing materials, works in
progress, supplies used in operations, and finished
goods.

IMF   **International Monetary Fund**
U.S. Government agency established in 1944 that
focuses on lowering trade barriers and stabilizing
currencies. The IMF has an international currency

called "special drawing rights" used to increase international liquidity.

IMF   **Inventory Master File**
Business management document or record, physical or electronic, that compiles all materials and items in inventory.

IMM   **International Monetary Market**
Division of the Chicago Mercantile Exchange (Merc) that trades futures in U.S. Treasury bills, foreign currencies, certificates of deposit and Eurodollar deposits. IMM publishes the *IMM Weekly Report*. The *Report* covers interest rate markets, gold and selected cash market information such as the prime rate and the federal funds.

IMM   **International Money Management**
Generic descriptor for practices and functions of conducting business and managing funds across international boundaries.

IMS   **Inventory Management System**
Business management term for systems and procedures, physical and electronic, involved with day-to-day management of the business' inventory, directed at maximizing profits by creating a strong balance between investment in inventory and smooth, continuous production.

IN   **Interest**
Cost of using money expressed as a rate per period of time.

IO   **Interest Only**
                  Banking term for a type of loan in which the only
                  current obligation is interest and repayment of the
                  principal is deferred.

IOP   **Initial Operating Period**
                  Business management term for time period (gen-
                  erally one year) considered a new business' start-
                  up period and in which financial performance
                  needs to be viewed differently.

IOU   **I Owe You**
                  Written acknowledgement of a debt, especially an
                  informal one, generally consisting only of the sum
                  owed and the names and signatures of the parties
                  involved.

IP   **Installment Paid**
                  Accounting and Bookkeeping term to indicate that
                  a specific installment on a long-term loan has been
                  paid in full.

IPE   **International Petroleum Exchange**
                  London-based energy futures and options
                  exchange.

IPO   **Initial Public Offering**
                  A corporation's first offering of stock to the
                  public.

IPRS   **Intellectual Property Rights**
                  The ownership of the right to posses or otherwise
                  use or dispose of products created by human
                  ingenuity.

IR **Investor Relations**
Internal function of an investment organization that is responsible for producing communication materials for the firm's clients and various publics.

IRA **Individual Retirement Account**
A personal, tax-deferred retirement account that an employed person can set up with deposits and their earnings tax-deferred under certain tax regulations.

IRB **Industrial Revenue Bond**
Interchangeable with Industrial Development Bond (IDB) and Industrial Development Revenue Bond (IDR).

IRC **Internal Revenue Code**
Term for the group of statutes and regulations comprising the federal tax law of the U.S.

IREF **International Real Estate Federation**
Paris-based organization offering programs and services for individuals and organizations involved or interested in international real estate investment.

IREM **Institute of Real Estate Management**
Chicago-based organization offering programs, products and services for property managers of all types of real estate, offers the Accredited Residential Manager (ARM) and Certified Property Manager (CPM) professional designations and publishes the *Journal of Property Management* (JPM).

Location:
IREM
430 N. Michigan Avenue
Chicago, IL 60611
(312) 329-6000

IRP

Interest Rate Parity

A state where the difference between national interest rates for securities of similar risk and maturity should be equal to but opposite in sign to the forward exchange rate differential between two currencies. The premium (P)/discount (D) are calculated as follows:

$$P \text{ (or D)} = \frac{r_f - r_d}{1 + r_f}$$

where r_f and r_d equal foreign and domestic interest rates.

IRPEG

Tax on Legal Entities

Italian taxation term.

IRR

Internal Rate of Return, also called time-adjusted rate of return

Discount rate at which the present value of the future cash flows of an investment equals the cost of the investment. The IRR formula is:

Initial Investment (I) = Present Value (PV), or Net Present Value (NPV) = 0
For example:

$$\$85,896 = \$4,000 \times PVIFA_{i,6}$$
$$PVIFA_{i,6} = \frac{\$85,896}{\$4,000} = 21.47$$

IRR is more exact than ARR because it considers the time value of money.

IRRC **Investor Responsibility Research Center (News for Investors)**
Monthly publication that monitors corporate conduct, shareholder resolutions among other issues of interest to investors. Published by:

Investor Responsibility Research Center
1755 Massachusetts Avenue, N.W.
Washington, D.C. 20046

IRS **Internal Revenue Service**
U.S. Government agency charged with collecting most federal taxes, administering U.S. Department of Treasury regulations, and investigating and resolving tax illegalities.

IRSC **Internal Revenue Service Center**
Any of a number of regional centers throughout the U.S. responsible for processing federal tax returns and refunds, and which serve as regional headquarters for IRS auditors and investigators.

IS **Income Statement**
Interchangeable with Profit and Loss (P&L) Statement, a summary of revenues, costs and expenses of a company during an accounting period.

I/S **Inventory to Sales Ratio**
Ratio that shows how many times the inventory of a business is sold during an accounting period.

ISCEBS **International Society of Certified Employee Benefit Specialists**

ISE   **International Stock Exchange of the United Kingdom (U.K.) and the Republic of Ireland**

ISO   **Incentive Stock Option**
Plan under which qualifying options are free of tax at the date of grant and the date of exercise, and profits on shares sold are subject to capital gains taxes depending on the length of time the shares are held.

ISRO   **International Securities Regulatory Organization**

IT   **Income Tax**
Annual tax on personal and corporate income levied by the U.S. federal government and by certain state and local governments.

ITA   **International Trade Administration**
Previously known as the U.S. Tariff Commission. Its primary objective is to oversee imports, import duties, and to assess the effect of foreign import structures on the U.S. economy.

ITA   **International Trade Association**
A department of the U.S. Department of Commerce. Offers assistance to U.S. exporters and businesses to be able to compete in the global marketplace.

ITC   **Investment Tax Credit**
Reduction in income tax liability granted by the federal government to firms making new investment in certain asset categories; also called Investment Credit (IC).

ITC   **International Trade Commission**
                A U.S. government agency whose function is to
                protect American interests in international trade.

ITF   **In Trust For**
                Financial management designation for assets held
                through a fiduciary relationship by one individual
                (trustee) for another (beneficiary).

IT/R   **Inventory Transfer Receipt**
                Bookkeeping term for documentation involved in
                transferring inventory from one location or
                account to another.

ITS   **Intermarket Trading System**
                Video/computer display system that links the posts
                of specialists at the New York, American, Boston,
                Midwest, Philadelphia and Pacific Stock
                Exchanges and NASD market makers who trade
                the same securities. A transaction that is accepted
                by a broker at one exchange is analogous to an
                "electronic handshake" and constitutes a contract.

IV   **Improved Value**
                Real estate term for a stated value of a property
                that includes both land and existing improvements
                (structures) thereon.

IVA   **Inventory Valuation Adjustment**
                Accounting and bookkeeping term for a revision
                to the valuation of one or more inventory items.

IWP   **Internal Working Paper**
                Accounting term for general notes and worksheets
                maintained as reference and background to an

accounting project and generally not included in the final documents.

J

JA   **Joint Account**
Financial management and banking term for a bank or brokerage account that is owned jointly by two or more people.

JAS   **Job Accounting System**
Accounting and systems management term for a computer system designed to compile and monitor costs and expense items on a project-by-project basis.

JIT   **Just In Time**
Business management term for inventory management and purchasing system whereby materials are ordered on an as-needed basis to minimize storage and other costs and to ensure that product is as up-to-date as possible.

JO   **Job Order**
Business management term for the documentation generated internally or between a customer and a supplier or vendor to establish the specifications and costs of a job or order.

JO   **Joint Ownership**
Business management. equal ownership by two or more people, generally who have right of survivorship.

JOA   **Joint Operating Agreement**
Business management. contract between two individuals or entities for the terms of shared operation of property or an enterprise or venture.

JS&A
(Advisory)   A newsletter published every three weeks which covers excerpts from other letters. Each issue includes one complete reprint of an excerpted letter.

JSE   **Johannesburg Stock Exchange**

JY   **Japanese Yen**
Monetary unit of Japan.

K

KCBT   **Kansas City Board of Trade**

KD   **Knocked Down**
Business management term for unassembled materials or merchandise.

L

LA   **Leasehold Area**
Real estate term for a detailed description and specifications of property in which a lessee or tenant has a lease, including how the leased area was measured.

LA   **Ledger Account**
                  Accounting and bookkeeping term for account
                  book(s) or records of final entry.

LA   **Liquid Asset**
                  Asset or property that can be quickly converted
                  into cash.

LAIS   **Loan Accounting Information System**
                  Accounting and systems management. computer
                  system designed to compile and monitor costs and
                  expense items on a loan-by-loan basis.

LAN   **Local Area Network**
                  Generally, a collection of microcomputers and
                  peripherals, such as hard disk drives and laser
                  printers, linked together by connections that pro-
                  vide cost-effective sharing of data and hardware
                  among all linked users who are usually all located
                  in the same building. There are three basic LAN
                  configurations:

                  1. Star, in which a central host computer has a
                     number of microcomputers wired to the host.
                  2. Ring, in which multiple computers are connect-
                     ed through a continuous communications cable
                     without a central computer.
                  3. Bus or Tree, in which a series of microcomput-
                     ers or peripherals are connected to a central
                     cable and to which other computers or peripher-
                     als can be added by tapping into the central
                     cable.

LBO   **Leveraged Buyout**
                  Business management and finance term for the
                  takeover of a company using borrowed funds, then
                  repaying the debt from the company's assets.

LC; L/C   **Letter of Credit**

Instrument or document issued by a bank guaranteeing the payment of a customer's drafts up to a stated amount for a specified time period. There are three primary L/Cs used in international trade that can be irrevocable or revocable and are summarized in the following table:

	Irrevocable	Irrevocable Confirmed L/C	Revocable Unconfirmed L/D
Who Applies	Importer	Importer	Importer
Who Pays	Issuing Bank and Confirming Bank	Issuing Bank	None
Who Applies for Amendment	Importer	Importer	Importer
Who Approves Amendment	Issuing Bank, Exporter, and Confirming Bank	Issuing Bank, and Exporter	Issuing Bank
Who Reimburses Paying Bank	Issuing Bank	Issuing Bank	Issuing Bank
Who Reimburses Issuing Bank	Importer	Importer	Importer

LC   **Line of Credit**

A bank's commitment to make loans to a particular customer up to a specified maximum amount during a specified time period.

LCE   **Latest Cost Estimate**

Accounting and Business term for most recent cost estimate on a specified item or project.

LCE   **London Commodity Exchange**

LCM   **Lower of Cost or Market**
Business term for the basis on which a price is set
being either the actual cost of the product or the
prevailing market price, whichever is lower.

LCO   **Lowest Cost of Ownership**
Business term for the lowest negotiable price for
owning an asset based on specified variables.

LDC   **Less Developed Country**
Subjective term for nation of relatively low
economic strength.

LDR   **Ledger**
Australian acronym for final book of accounting
entry.

LE   **Latest Estimate**
Most recent estimate of price on specified goods
or services.

LESOP   **Leveraged Employee Stock Ownership Plan**
Business term for an employee stock ownership
plan (ESOP) in which employee pension and
profit-sharing plans borrow money to purchase
stock in the company.

LESS   **Least Cost Estimating and Scheduling
System**
Business. planning model that aims to schedule
use of resources at minimal costs.

LGR   **Leasehold Ground Rent**
Real estate term for the rental income earned by
leased unimproved land.

LIFFE   **London International Financial Futures and Options Exchange**

LIFO   **Last In, First Out**
                   Inventory accounting method related to FIFO.

LIBOR   **London Interbank Offered Rate**
                   The deposit on interbank transactions in the eurocurrency market. The rate is used as a base for many international interest rate transactions.

LILO   **Last In, Last Out**
                   Inventory accounting term.

LINC   **Licensed Independent Network of CPA Financial Planners**
                   Network of CPA/PFS fee-only planners in public accounting firms. Contact at (800) 737-2727.

LISH; LIST   **Last In, Still Here; Last In, Still There**
                   Facetious terms as variations on LIFO and FIFO inventory accounting methods, referring to inventory that hasn't sold as quickly as anticipated.

LL   **Low Load**
                   Mutual fund investment that is sold for a relatively low sales charge.

LLC   **Limited Liability Corporation**
                   Type of corporate entity, not available in all 50 of the United States, that combines the tax and legal characteristics of organization as a corporation and as a partnership.

LMM **Liquid Money Market**
Money-market investment that can be quickly converted to cash.

LMRA **Labor-Management Relations Act**
Also known as Taft-Hartley Act, passed into U.S. law in 1947 and the provisions of which include injunctions against labor strikes.

LN **Lien**
A creditor's claim against an individual's or entity's property or assets.

LN **Loan**
Transaction wherein one party allows a second party to use property or assets for a specified period of time, generally in exchange for payment (interest).

LN **Lot Number**
Business management term for a group of goods or services assigned a unique number for identification purposes.

LO **Lowest Offer**
Business management term for the smallest amount offered in exchange for goods or services for sale.

LOB **Line of Business**
Descriptor for type of goods or services offered by a business or individual.

LP **Limited Partnership**
Organization established to manage a business or project, composed of general partners to manage

the venture and limited partners who invest with-out liability and without involvement in day-to-day operations.

LP   **Linear Programming**
A technique that maximizes a revenue, contribu-tion or profit function, or minimizes a cost func-tion. Linear Programming has two components:

1. Objective function
2. Constraints, including nonnegativity con-straints, which are typically inequalities.

LPS   **Last Period Satisfied**
IRS term as indicator for the most recent tax peri-od for which a taxpayer's obligations are paid in full.

LR   **Low Risk**
Descriptor for project or investment evaluated as holding little possibility of having little or no return on investment.

LR   **Loan Rate**
Percentage (generally annual) of interest applied to a loan.

LS   **Lump Sum**
Single large payment of money paid or received as opposed to periodic payments.

LSC   **Lump-Sum Contract**
Business agreement setting forth terms for pay-ment or repayment of an obligation in a single amount .

LSD   **Lump-Sum Distribution**
                      Single payment made to a departing or retiring
                      employee covering pension, salary reduction
                      and/or profit-sharing plans, and to which certain
                      tax rules apply.

LT   **Legal Tender**
                      Currency that may be lawfully offered or accepted
                      in purchases or in payments of debts.

LTD   **Limited**
                      A British business formed as a corporation.

LTCG   **Long-Term Capital Gain**
                      Profits on the sale of an asset held for longer than
                      12 months and subject to long-term capital gain
                      taxes.

LTCL   **Long-Term Capital Loss**
                      Loss on the sale of an asset held for longer than 12
                      months and which can for tax purposes be used to
                      offset capital gains and ordinary income.

LTP   **Limit on Tax Preferences**
                      IRS limitation on amounts of certain items, such as
                      passive losses and depreciation, that can be used as
                      deductions when calculating Alternative
                      Minimum Tax (AMT).

LTV   **Loan to Value Ratio**
                      Ratio of money borrowed to fair market value of
                      the property involved, usually real estate.

LV   **Land Value**
                      Real estate term for market value of unimproved
                      land or the underlying land of improved property.

LWOP   **Leave Without Pay**
                  Business term for approved leave of absence for
                  an employee during which no salary is drawn.

LWP   **Leave With Pay**
                  Business term for approved leave of absence for
                  an employee during which all or partial salary is
                  drawn.

M

M-1   **Currency in circulation**
                  Money supply such as commercial bank demand
                  deposits, traveler's checks, credit union share
                  drafts, NOW and automatic transfer from savings
                  (ATS), and mutual savings bank demand deposits.

M-2   **M-1**
                  Money supply. Components include M-1 plus
                  overnight Eurodollars and repurchase agreements
                  issued by commercial banks, savings accounts,
                  money market mutual fund shares, and time
                  deposits under $100,000.

M-3   **M-2**
                  Money supply that includes the components of M-
                  2 and time deposits over $100,000 and term repur-
                  chase agreements.

MA   **Margin Account**
                  Investment account that allows a customer to buy
                  securities with money borrowed from the broker
                  under certain terms.

M&A   **Mergers and Acquisitions**
Combination of two or more companies (merger)
or the takeover by one company of the controlling
interest of another (acquisition); specialized area
of financial management and consulting.

MACRS   **Modified Accelerated Cost Recovery System**
Taxation rules for the depreciation of qualifying
assets set forth in the Tax Reform Act of 1986.

MAF   **Master Appraisal File**
Real estate term for compilation of key data for
appraisals of a certain property type or class in a
given area.

MAS   **Management Accounting System**
Generic term for computer and related systems
directed towards business operations and decision-
making.

MAS   **Management Advisory Services**
Business management and consulting services
offered by accountants, generally in the areas of
computer technology, budgeting, internal controls,
operations, planning, human resources and other
management decision-making functions.

MB   **Merchant Bank**
European or U.S. financial institution that offers
services that include investment banking, portfolio
management, mergers and acquisitions, and
accepting deposits generated by bank credit/debit
and charge card transactions.

MB   **Municipal Bond**
Tax-exempt bonds issued by municipalities, usually for public improvement or operating budgets.

MBB   **Mortgage-Backed Bonds**
Securities backed by mortgages. The Government National Mortgage Association (GNMA) guarantees some of the mortgages.

MBO   **Management Buyout**
Purchase of all of a company's publicly held shares by existing management, thereby taking the company private.

MBR   **Maximum Base Rent**
Real estate term for the level above which a property's base rent (excluding add-on fees, etc.) cannot rise during the stated term of the lease.

MBS   **Mortgage-Backed Securities**
Interchangeable with Mortgage-Backed Bonds (MBB).

MC   **Marginal Cost**
Business management term for the change in the total costs of an enterprise as the result of one more or one less unit of output, also called incremental cost. Formula:

$$MC = \frac{\text{Change in total cost}}{\text{Change in quantity}}$$

MCA   **Material Control Adjustment**
Revision of current or planned inventory or production as a means to optimize material purchases.

MCC   **Marginal Cost of Capital**
Analysis that relates a firm's cost of capital to the level of new financing, used to determine the discount rate to be used in the firm's capital budgeting process:

1. Determine the cost and the percentage of financing to be used for each source of capital (e.g., debt, preferred stock, and common stock equity.)
2. Use the following formula to compute the points where the weighted cost will increase:

Break point = Maximum amount of the lower cost source of capital / Percentage of financing provided by the source

3. Calculate the weighted cost of capital over the range of total financing between break points.
4. Construct a table that shows the weighted cost of capital for each level of total new financing.

MCE   **Manufacturing Cycle Effectiveness**
Business management measure, expressed as a percentage, of the efficacy of a specified manufacturing process.

MD   **Maturity Date**
Investment term for (1) date on which the principal amount of a dept instrument becomes due and payable; (2) date on which an installment loan must be paid in full; (3) average due date of factored receivables.

MD   **Memorandum of Deposit**
Banking documentation for cash, checks or drafts placed with a financial institution for credit to an account.

MD   **Money Down**
Down payment on a loan under contract.

M&D   **Mergers and Divestitures**
Combination of two or more companies (merger) or the disposition of the controlling interest of one company by another (divestiture) through outright sale, employee purchase, liquidation, etc.; specialized area of financial management and consulting.

ME   **Math Error**
Accounting and IRS term used to indicate where a calculation has been found to contain an arithmetic error.

MERC   **Chicago Mercantile Exchange**
See CME.

MGN   **Margin**
Brokerage and investment term for the amount that an investor deposits with a broker when borrowing from the broker to buy securities.

MHA   **Man-Hour Accounting**
Accounting system that emphasizes labor hours and related costs connected with a specific job or project.

MIBOR   **Madrid Interbank Offered Rate**
International banking term.

MIC   **Material Inventory Control**
Accounting and bookkeeping systems for monitoring material, from raw material to finished goods.

MIF   **Master Inventory File**
                   Accounting and bookkeeping term for primary
                   documents and recordkeeping systems for
                   material inventory.

MIF   **Mercato Italiano Futures**
                   Italian Futures Market

MIMS   **Material Information Management System**
                   Accounting and management term for computer-
                   ized and other systems for managing and reporting
                   on the material components of a business.

MIPO   **Multiple-Item Purchase Order**
                   Bookkeeping and management document setting
                   forth the specifications and terms for an order
                   between customer and vendor of more than one
                   item.

MIR   **Master Inventory Record**
                   Accounting and bookkeeping term for primary
                   documents and records for material inventory.

MIS   **Management Information Systems**
                   Business management term for aggregate of inter-
                   nal business functions encompassing all technolo-
                   gy-related processing and reporting.

MIT   **Market-If-Touched Order**
                   A contingent buy/sell order of securities at market
                   price if execution of another order is placed at a
                   given price.

MIT   **Municipal Investment Trust**
                   Investment trust that buys municipal bonds and
                   passes the tax-free income on to shareholders.

MLP   **Master Limited Partnership**
Public limited partnership composed of certain types of corporate assets or private limited partnerships, especially used for real estate or oil and gas ventures.

MLS   **Multiple Listing Service**
Association of real estate agents who agree to share property listings with one another and share commissions among two or more agents who participate in a completed transaction.

MM   **Money Market**
Market for short-term debt instruments.

MMDA   **Money Market Deposit Account**
Highly liquid, market-sensitive bank account available since 1982, with an interest rate generally comparable to rates on money-market mutual funds, and insured by the Federal Deposit Insurance Corporation.

MMF   **Money Market Fund**
Open-ended mutual fund that invests in highly liquid and safe securities and pays commensurate interest rates.

MMMF   **Money Market Mutual Fund**
Interchangeable with but less often used than Money Market Fund (MMF).

MNC   **Multinational Corporation**
A corporation operating in more than one country but owned only in one country.

MNE   **Multinational Enterprise**
                Business entity conducting business internationally.

MOI   **Minimum Operating Inventory**
                Lowest or smallest amount of material needed to maintain a business or a certain process.

MONEP   **Marche des Options Negociables de Paris**
                Subsidiary of Paris Bourse, the national stock market of France.

MOP   **Margin of Profit**
                Accounting and business term for net sales less cost of goods. relationship between gross profits and net sales.

MP   **Market Price**
                Price agreed upon by willing buyers and sellers of a product or service as determined by supply and demand. Brokerage. last reported price at which a security was sold on an exchange.

M/P   **Mail Payment**
                Bookkeeping indicator of how a payment was or will be made or received.

MSCI EAFE   **Morgan Stanley Capital International Europe Australia Far East Index**
                The index tracks the performance of all major stock markets outside of North America. It is market-weighted and is composed of 1,041 companies. It is the major index used by investors to see how U.S. shares are performing against other markets worldwide.

MTN   **Medium-Term Note**
                 Note with a maturity of two to ten years.

MTR   **Marginal Rate of Tax**
                 Tax rate paid on the last dollar of income earned;
                 the highest tax rate paid.

MTSR   **Mid-Term Status Report**
                 Management report produced at the halfway point
                 of a financial reporting period or a project's com-
                 pletion timeline, scheduled to evaluate the condi-
                 tion of the project.

MU   **Markup**
                 Cost difference between a retailer's costs for a
                 product or service and what the retailer charges
                 customers.

MUD   **Mixed Use Development**
                 Real estate term for property planned and/or zoned
                 for different types of buildings, *e.g.*, residential
                 and commercial.

MUD   **Municipal Utility District**
                 Political subdivision within a municipality that
                 provides utility-related services and may issue
                 special assessment bonds.

MURB   **Multi-Unit Residential Building**
                 Canadian real estate term for apartment building.

MV   **Market Value**
                 Theoretical highest price that a willing buyer
                 would pay for a product or service, and lowest
                 price that a willing seller would accept, both
                 parties acting fully informed and intelligently.

MWL   **Minimum Wage Laws**
Federal legislation that sets forth the lowest fixed wage payable to employees of various groups.

MXD   **Mixed Use District**
Real estate term for land planned and/or zoned for a variety of uses, *e.g.*, residential and commercial.

N

NA   **Net Assets**
Total assets of a business less liabilities.

NA   **Not Applicable or Not Available**
Used in many contexts as indicator of information, material or product either unavailable or irrelevant.

NABE   **National Association of Business Economists**
Conducts a survey on the future economic condition of the nation.

NADS   **Net After Debt Service**
Gross profit less annual debt service (ADS).

NAR   **National Association of Realtors**
Trade organization for education and professional services to the real estate industry.

U.S. headquarters:
430 N. Michigan Ave.
Chicago, IL 60611
(321) 329-8200

NAREIT **National Association of Real Estate Investment Trusts**
Trade organization representing the interests of those involved in Real Estate Investment Trusts.

Location:
1129 Twentieth St., N.W.
Washington, D.C. 20036

NASD **National Association of Securities Dealers**
New-York based organization for standards and ethical behavior composed of investment banking firms and supervised by the Securities Exchange Commission (SEC). NASD monitors the over-the-counter (OTC) market.

NASDAQ **National Association of Securities Dealers Automated Quotations System**
Computerized system owned by NASD, listing prices for over-the-counter securities. NASDAQ currently lists over 5,500 stocks with a total market capitalization of over $1.6 trillion.

NAV **Net Asset Value**
Market value of a mutual fund share. NAV is measured as follows:

NAV = Fund's total assets - Liabilities
          Number of shares outstanding in the fund

For example, let's look at AAA mutual fund:

AAA Mutual Fund	*Market Value*
Value of the portfolio	$38,000
Minus total liabilities	$12,000
Net Value	$26,000
Number of shares outstanding	2,000
NAV per share ($26,000 ، 2,000)	$13.00

To determine the value of an investment assuming 5% or 100 shares of the fund's outstanding shares are owned, simple multiply the NAV by the number of shares held. Thus, the value of the investment is:

$13.00 x 100 = $1,300

NB

Nonbusiness
Tax-accounting indicator for personal as opposed to business-related income or expenses.

NBER

National Bureau of Economic Research
Publishers of the Business Conditions Digest. The bureau analyzes and selects the time series data based on each series' ability to be identified as a leading, coincident or lagging indicator over several decades of aggregate economic activity. The Digest can be used to understand past economic behavior and to forecast future economic activity with a high degree of accuracy.

NBH

National Bank of Hungary

NBR

Nightly Business Report
Television program that provides consumer, business and financial news.

NC

No Charge
Accounting and bookkeeping term to indicate waiver of all or certain parts of costs for a product or service.

NC

Noncollectable
Accounting and bookkeeping term to indicate an invoice or receivable amount that the business has

unsuccessfully attempted to collect and subsequently determined to be lost.

NCI   **No-Cost Item**
Business inventory item with no or insignificant cost to the business and/or given to customers at no charge.

NCI   **No Currency Involved**
International transaction in which no money was exchanged between the parties.

NCV   **No Commercial Value**
Business product, service or commodity determined to have no current value in any market.

ND   **National Debt**
Economics term for all debt owned by a federal government.

ND   **Net Debt**
Finance term for total debt owed by an individual or business entity.

NDB   **Net Debt Balance**
Finance term for total current unpaid principal amount on a loan.

NE   **Net Earnings**
Finance term for income remaining after all expenses have been paid or deducted.

nd   **Next Day**
Indicator of requirement for next day delivery of stock certificates, and for settlement (payment) on that same day.

NF   **No Funds**
                  Banking and bookkeeping indicator for an account
                  with no current deposits.

NFA   **National Futures Association**
                  National organization representing and serving the
                  interests of those involved in the futures markets.

                  Location:
                  National Futures Association
                  200 W. Madison Avenue, Suite 1600
                  Chicago, IL 60606
                  (312) 781-1300

NICS   **Newly Industrialized Countries**
                  Economics term for nations recently converted
                  and/or newly introduced to methods and aims of
                  industrialization.

NIF   **Note Issuance Facility**
                  Facility provided by a syndicate of banks allowing
                  borrowers to issue short-term notes that are placed
                  by the syndicate in the eurocurrency markets.

NIS   **Not In Stock**
                  Inventory management term for product or item
                  not currently available for use or purchase.

NL   **No Load**
                  Mutual fund with no commission or sales charge.

NOI   **Net Operating Income**
                  Gross income from operating a property or busi-
                  ness less operating expenses, but before deducting
                  income taxes and financing expenses.

NOL   **Net Operating Loss**
Accounting term for excess of business expenses over income in a tax year.

NOP   **Non-Operating**
Business and accounting term for any source of income or expense other than direct operation function of the business.

NOW   **Negotiable Order of Withdrawal Account**
Bank or savings and loan account on which negotiable withdrawal drafts can be written; an interest-bearing checking account.

NP   **Nonprofit, Not-for-Profit**
Organization exempt from corporate income taxes, generally operated for charitable, humanitarian or educational purposes, and to which donations are tax-deductible by the donor.

NP   **Notary Public**
Public officer or other person authorized to authenticate contracts, acknowledge deeds, take affidavits, etc.

NP   **Notes Payable**
Finance term for a written promise to pay a specified amount to a certain entity on demand or on a specified date, reflected as a liability on the financial statement.

NPV   **Net Present Value**
Investment analysis method of determining whether performance of a proposed investment will be adequate for the investor's objectives. The present value (PV) of all cash inflows from the

investment is compared to the initial investment. Formula:

NPV = PV − I

If the result is an NPV > 1, an investment is worthy of consideration.

NR; N/R   **Not Rated**
Indicator used by securities rating services and mercantile agencies for securities or companies that have not been rated, and having neither a positive nor negative implication.

N/R   **Notes Receivable**
Finance term for a written promise to receive payment of a specified amount on demand or on a specified date, reflected as an asset on the financial statement.

NRA   **Net Rentable Area**
Real estate term for that portion of space in a building or project that may be rented to tenants and upon which rental payments are based.

NSCC   **National Securities Clearing Corporation**
Organization through which brokerage firms, exchanges and other clearing corporations reconcile accounts with each other.

NSE   **Nigerian Stock Exchange**

NSF   **Not Sufficient Funds**
Draft or note not payable because the account on which it is drawn has insufficient funds to cover the amount written.

NT

Net Tax
Total tax owed after all deductions, exemptions and adjustments to income.

N/T

Net Terms
Amount owed after all relevant deductions have been taken from the gross amount.

NTA

Net Tangible Assets
Total assets of a company less any intangible assets, *e.g.*, goodwill, patents and trademarks, and less all liabilities.

NTDB

National Trade Data Bank
An international trade data bank compiled by 15 U.S. Government agencies. The data bank contains the latest census data on U.S. imports and exports by commodity and country, the complete *CIA World Factbook*, and current market research among others. Information can be obtained from:

U.S. Department of Commerce
14th and Constitution Avenue, N.W.
Washington, D.C. 20230
202-482-1986

NVS

Non-Voting Stock
Securities that do not empower the holder to vote on corporate resolutions or the election of directors.

NW

Net Worth
The value of all assets of an individual or organization minus any debts.

NWC

Net Working Capital
Current assets minus current liabilities.

NYCE	**New York Cotton Exchange**
NYF, NYFE	**New York Futures Exchange**
NYME, NYMEX	**New York Mercantile Exchange**
NYSE	**New York Stock Exchange**

Also called the *Big Board* and *The Exchange*, the NYSE was established in 1792 and is the oldest and largest stock exchange in the U.S. It is located at:

New York Stock Exchange
11 Wall Street
New York, NY 10005
212-656-3000

NZSE	**New Zealand Stock Exchange**

O

OA **Office Audit**
Accounting term for a professional examination and verification of accounts and records and supporting data, and a report or statement of the results of the examination, for an individual office of a company.

OA **Old Account**
Account inactive but kept open.

OA **On Account**
Accounting term for the partial payment of an obligation; an informal transaction in which a

buyer agrees to make payment at some time after goods are delivered.

OA   **Open Account**
Accounting term for a credit account with an unpaid balance.

OAC   **On Approved Credit**
Goods or services delivered based on the customer's credit previously approved by the vendor.

OB   **Obligation Bond**
Mortgage bond in which the face value exceeds the value of the underlying property, and the difference compensates the lender for its costs exceeding the mortgage value.

OB   **Operating Budget**
Estimate of revenue and expenditure involving the direct operation of an enterprise for a specified period.

OB   **Out of Business**
Indicator of client or customer that has ceased operation.

OBL   **Outstanding Balance List**
Accounting report listing all unpaid amounts in a certain time period and/or for a certain division.

OBR   **Office of Budget and Reports**
U.S. Government agency.

OBRA   **Office of Business Research and Analysis**
U.S. Department of Commerce agency.

OC   **Open Contract**
                Agreement whose terms have not been fully nego-
                tiated, executed or completed.

OCC   **Options Clearing Corporation**
                Corporation owned by stock exchanges, handling
                options transactions.

OD   **Overdraft, Overdrawn**
                Extension of credit by a lending institution on a
                draft or check written on an account.

OE   **Operating Expense**
                Expenditure directly related to producing a
                product or service.

OEBS   **Office of Employee Benefits Security**
                U.S. Department of Labor subsidiary.

OECD   **Organization for Economic Cooperation and
                Development**
                An organization addresses issues of mutual con-
                cern with a view of expanding foreign trade, eco-
                nomic growth, and employment. The organization
                is composed of countries including the United
                States, England, France, Germany, Canada, Japan,
                Greece, and Australia

OEEO   **Office of Equal Employment Opportunity**
                U.S. Department of Labor subsidiary.

OEIT   **Open-End Investment Trust**
                Trust that continually creates new investment
                shares on demand.

OEX   **Options Exchange**
Location where option securities are traded.

OFLT   **Office of Foreign Labor and Trade**
U.S. Department of Commerce subsidiary.

OI   **Operating Income**
Revenue directly related to the product or service
that a business offers.

OID   **Original Issue Discount**
Bond bought at a deep discount, also called a
Zero-Coupon Bond. The interest is added to the
principal semiannually and both the principal and
the accumulated interest are paid at maturity.

OL   **Operating Loss**
The difference between the revenues of a business
and the related costs and expenses, excluding
income derived from sources other than regular
activities and before income deductions, where
costs and expenses exceed revenues.

OM   **Options Market**
Aggregate of people and exchanges involved in
buying and selling options securities.

OLTP   **On-Line Transaction Processing**
Systems involved in electronic processing of
investment sales and purchases.

OMB   **Office of Management and Budget**
Federal agency in the executive branch.

OMO   **Ordinary Money Order**
Financial instrument that can be easily converted
into cash by the payee named on the order.

OPBU   **Operating Budget**
Estimate of revenue and expenditure involving the
direct operation of an enterprise for a specified
period.

O/PD   **Overpaid**
Indicator for an amount paid exceeding the
amount due or billed.

OPM   **Other People's Money**
Borrowed funds.

OPM   **Options Pricing Model**
An option pricing model. Developed in 1973 by
Fischer Black and Myron Scholes, the model is
used to price OTC options and value option portfolios. The five factors determining the premium
of an option's market value over its expiration
value are:

1. Time to maturity
2. Stock price volatility
3. Exercise price
4. Stock price
5. Risk-free rate

The formula is:

$$V = P[N(d_1)] - Xe^{-rt}[N(d_2)]t$$

where V = current value of a call option
         P = current price of the underlying stock

N(d) = cumulative normal probability density function = probability that a deviation less *d* will occur in a standard normal distribution.

X = exercise or strike price of the option

t = time to exercise date

r = risk-free rate of interest (continuously compounded)

e = 2.71828

$$d_1 = \frac{\ln(P / X) + [r + s^2 / 2]t}{s \sqrt{t}}$$

$$d_2 = \frac{\ln(P / X) + [r + s^2 / 2]t}{s \sqrt{t}}$$

or

$$d_1 - s \sqrt{t}$$

s^2 = variance per period of rate of stock return (continuously compounded)

O/S　　**Outstanding**

Accounting and bookkeeping indicator of financial or other obligation unfulfilled.

OSE　　**Osaka (Japan) Stock Exchange**

OSHA　　**Occupational Safety and Health Act**

Federal legislation of 1970 regarding employers' responsibilities for safety and health in the workplace.

OSI　　**Out of Stock, Indefinite**

Indicator of a product or inventory item unavailable for an undetermined period of time but not discontinued.

OST   **Out of Stock, Temporary**
Indicator of a product or inventory item unavailable but due to be restocked.

OT   **Overtime**
Time during which an employee worked before or after regularly scheduled working times, pay for which is at the employee's regular hourly wage.

OTC   **Over the Counter**
Securities that are not listed and traded on a national exchange, but are traded electronically through brokers; sometimes called the Third Market.

OTP   **Overtime Premium**
Time during which an employee worked before or after regularly scheduled working times, pay for which is higher than the employee's regular hourly wage.

OTS   **Office of Thrift Supervision**
U.S. Treasury Department subsidiary established in 1989.

P

PA   **Public Accountant**
Accountant offering services to the public at large as opposed to one employed on a full-time basis by a company, but not having met statutory and

licensing requirements to obtain certification as a CPA.

PA **Purchasing Agent**
Individual carrying out the function in a company of managing purchases of goods and services and relationships with vendors, to maintain compliance with company standards and obtain economies of scale and other advantages.

PAL **Passive Activity Loss**
Loss produced by investment activities (such as a limited partnership) in which the investor does not materially participate, carrying certain tax consequences.

PAL **Pre-Approved Loan**
Lending arrangement in which the borrower has been qualified by the lender to obtain a loan of certain terms within a certain time period.

PAM **Pledged Account Mortgage**
Real estate mortgage loan in which part of the down-payment funds are "pledged" to the lender and placed in an interest-bearing account, and drawn from over time to help pay down the mortgage.

PAP **Pre-Arranged Payments**
Schedule agreed upon between a customer and vendor or borrower and lender by which certain payments occur automatically.

PAT **Pre-Arranged Transfers**
Schedule agreed upon between two or more parties by which funds or materials are moved among

accounts automatically in order to accomplish stated objectives.

PBGC   **Pension Benefit Guaranty Corporation**
Federal corporation that guarantees basic pension benefits in covered plans by administering terminated plans and placing liens on corporate assets for certain pension liabilities that were not funded.

PBP   **Pay-Back Period**
Amount of time required for the cumulative estimated future income from an investment to equal the amount initially invested.

PBR   **Price to Book Value**
Ratio of the market value of a company's stock to its tangible net worth.

PC   **Plus Commissions**
Indicator that a specified amount does not include commission fees.

PC   **Petty Cash**
Small cash fund maintained by a business for paying minor expenses such as office supplies, delivery gratuities, etc.

PCA   **Personal Cash Allowance**
Amount budgeted for an individual's discretionary expenses such as entertaining.

PCS   **Preferred Capital Stock**
Generally referred to simply as Preferred Stock, a class of stock that pays dividends usually at a fixed rate and that has priority over common stock in the receipt of dividend income and liquidation of

assets, and which generally does not carry voting rights.

PD   **Past Due**
Indicator of an invoice or other indebtedness unpaid as of its due date as specified in the credit terms.

PD   **Per Diem**
Daily allowance, usually for incidental expenses while traveling for business.

PD   **Post-Dated**
Check, letter, invoice, document, etc., dated later than the date on which it was actually written.

PDA   **Payroll Deduction Authorization**
Documentation between an employee and employer setting forth one-time or ongoing deductions from salary or wages for, *e.g.*, tax withholding, employee benefits, etc.

PDD   **Past Due Date**
Indicator or payment received after due date or remaining unpaid after due date.

PDE (Tape)   **Price-Dividend-Earnings Tape**
Contains monthly data on per share performance. One of the CompuStat tapes developed by Investors Management Science Company, a subsidiary of Standard & Poor's Corporation.

PDI   **Personal Disposable Income**
Individual income in excess of needs for living expenses and taxes, and therefore discretionary for investment, entertainment, etc.

PE   **Period Ending**
                          Accompanied by a date, indicates termination date
                          of a specified financial reporting, interest-earning,
                          or billing period.

P/E. PER   **Price/Earnings Ratio**
                          Also called *earnings multiple*, the P/E ratio repre-
                          sents the amount investors are willing to pay for
                          each dollar of the firm's earnings. A high multiple
                          shows that investors are positive on the firm. The
                          formula is:

                          Price/earnings ratio = Market price per share
                                                          Earnings per share

                          For example, assume the following:

                          • Firm's market price on Dec. 31, 19X1 = $14.00
                            and earnings per share = $1.80
                          • Firm's market price on Dec. 31, 19X2 = $28.00
                            and earnings per share = $2.10

                          Then:

                          P/E 19X1 = $14.00 = 7.78
                                       $1.80

                          P/E 19X2 = $28.00 = 13.33
                                       $2.10

                          Thus, investors are showing a higher opinion of
                          the firm in Year 2.

PED   **Period End Date**
                          Indicates last calendar date of a specified financial
                          reporting or billing period.

PEFCO   **Private Export Funding Corporation**
                          Established with U.S. Government support,
                          PEFCO is a private corporation that help finance

U.S. exports. Private capital is raised to fund export big-ticket items by American firms by purchasing medium- to long-term debt obligations of importers of U.S. goods at fixed interest rates.

PEP   **Paperless Electronic Payment**
Indicator of payment made generally by telephone or computer, often automatically on a specified due date, and without cash or check.

PERCS   **Preferred Equity—Redemption Cumulative Stock**
Form of preferred stock that allows holders of shares of common stock to exchange common stock for preferred shares, thereby retaining a higher dividend rate.

PERLS   **Principal Exchange-Rate-Linked Securities**
U.S. debt instrument that pays interest with principal repayment linked to performance of the U.S. dollar vs. foreign currency.

PERT   **Program Evaluation and Review Technique**
Management tool that involves diagrammatic representations of the activities comprising a project and the sequence of those activities, using arrows for tasks that are distinct segments requiring time and resources and circles for milestone points or completed events that do not consume any time in themselves. *See also* CPMI—Critical Path Method.

PF   **Pension Fund**
Fund established by a corporation or other organization to pay post-retirement non-wage benefits to employees or their designated beneficiaries.

pf **Preferred Stock**
Class of capital stock that pays dividends at a specified rate and that has preference over common stock in the payment of dividends and liquidation of assets, but that generally does not have voting rights.

PGIM **Potential Gross Income Multiplier**
Ratio of the value of a piece of real estate to the income the property could potentially generate, used as a rule-of-thumb indicator of the property's viability as an investment.

PI **Personal Income**
Income received by an individual from all sources.

PI **Prime Interest Rate**
Base rate used by banks in pricing commercial loans to their most creditworthy customers, generally used as a bellwether rate throughout the lending community.

P&I **Principal and Interest**
Indicates that an amount paid includes both repayment of principal and interest per the lending terms.

PIG **Passive Income Generator**
Investment vehicle intended to generate passive income (*i.e.*, investor does not materially participate in the activities of the investment) as a source of tax-sheltered income.

PIK **Payment In Kind**
Payment for goods and services with other goods and services rather than cash or securities; invest-

ments, bonds or preferred stock that pays interest or dividends in the form of additional bonds or shares of preferred stock.

PIL **Payment In Lieu**
Payment for goods and services in cash or securities rather than goods or services as agreed upon.

PIN **Personal Identification Number**
Number, generally selected by the customer, used to access funds or account information electronically.

PIP **Payment In Part**
Indicator of partial payment of an invoice or other amount due.

PIP **Profit Improvement Program**
Plan to increase the profitability of a product or service through a combination of maximizing sales or other revenue, and managing costs.

PITI **Principal, Interest, Taxes (property) and Insurance**
Real estate term for monthly payment required for a home mortgage loan.

PJ **Purchases Journal**
Bookkeeping system in which all purchases are recorded before posting in the ledger.

P/L, P&L **Profit and Loss**
Summary of revenues, costs and expenses of a business entity during a financial reporting period.

PL   **Price List**
Reference summary of current prices charged for products and services, including information on discounts, etc.

PMI   **Private Mortgage Insurance**
Insurance on a conventional mortgage loan that indemnifies the lender from the borrower's default.

PO   **Purchase Order**
Documentation between a customer and vendor setting forth the specifications of an order for goods, including terms of delivery and payment.

PP   **Pay Period**
Payroll management indicator of time period for which salaries and wages are paid.

PP   **Personal Property**
Assets (tangible and intangible) other than real estate.

PPBS   **Program-Planning-Budgeting System**
Planning-oriented approach to developing a budget in which expenditures are based primarily on programs of work and secondarily on character and object. The value of PPBS lies in the process of making program policy decisions that lead to a specific budget and plans for each year in which the program will run.

PPD   **Pre-Paid**
Indicator that costs for goods or services purchased have been or must be paid before delivery.

PPI   **Producer Price Index**
Measure of the cost of a given basket of goods priced in wholesale markets, including raw materials, semifinished goods and finished goods, released monthly by the Bureau of Labor Statistics (U.S. Department of Commerce), signaling changes in the general price level or Consumer Price Index (CPI).

PR   **Payroll**
Records of employees to be paid and the amount due to each, the total of these amounts, funds to be paid out, and general processing and management involved in this function.

PRD   **Payroll Deduction**
Withholding from salary and other compensation to provide for an individual's tax liability, employee benefits, etc.

PS   **Profit Sharing**
Agreement between a corporation and its employees that allows employees to participate in the profits of the business.

PSE   **Pacific Stock Exchange**
A regional stock exchange, based in both Los Angeles and San Francisco, that handles trading on the West Coast.

PT   **Payment**
Record-keeping indicator of an amount received corresponding with an amount owed.

PT   **Perfect Title**
                 Generally referred to as Clear Title, indicating that
                 title to a property is free of disputed interests.

PT   **Profit Taking**
                 Cashing in short-term securities or commodities
                 on gains earned in a sharp market rise.

PT   **Purchase Tax**
                 British tax.

PTE   **Pre-Tax Earnings**
                 Earnings or profits before federal income taxes.

PTY.LTD   **Proprietary Limited**
                 A term used in Australia, Singapore, and other
                 countries for an owned corporation.

PUM   **Per Unit Per Month.**
                 Refers to monthly revenue or expenses associated
                 with each unit of production.

PV   **Present Value**
                 The value today of an amount to be received in the
                 future based on a compound interest rate. (*See*
                 IRR—Internal Rate of Return)

PVIF   **Present Value Interest Factor**
                 In real estate, the compound interest rate used in
                 discounting the projected future value of an invest-
                 ment back to its present value.

PVIF   **Present Value Interest Factor of an Annuity**
                 The interest rate used in discounting the total
                 income stream of an annuity to its present value.

PW　　　　　**Per Week**
Indicator of accounting of tabulating costs or other occurrences on a weekly basis.

PY　　　　　**Prior Year**
Refers to inclusion of financial information for the previous fiscal year or the same reporting period in the previous fiscal year, for comparison purposes.

PYR　　　　**Prior Year Report**
Financial or other management reports for the previous fiscal year for comparison purposes.

Q

Q　　　　　**Quarter; Quarterly**

QB　　　　　**Qualified Buyer**

QC　　　　　**Quality Control**
Any process a business uses to ensure that its product or service has a consistently high quality, using inspections, customer feedback and other tools at various points and times.

QOR　　　　**Quarterly Operating Report**
Financial and other management information compiled every three months.

QP　　　　　**Quadratic Programming**
Special class of mathematical programming similar to linear programming, quadratic programming is most often and best applied to models directed at minimizing some measure of risk associated

with a portfolio while maximizing return on the total investment, the objective being to determine the amount of funds to commit to each security from among a number of potential securities.

QPRT **Qualified Personal Residence Trust**
An estate-planning mechanism in which the owner of a personal residence (which can include a vacation home) transfers a remainder interest in the property to his descendants or other named beneficiaries, reserving a right to occupy and use the residence for a specified term. The present value of the reserved right, determined by application of government-provided factors, can be subtracted from the value of the property at the time of the gift in order derive the federal gift tax (FGT) value of the transfer. If the transferor dies before the term use interest expires, the value of the entire property at the transferor's death is taxed as part of the entire estate for federal estate tax (FET) purposes.

QVEC **Qualified Voluntary Employee Contribution**
Generally ongoing employee-initiated payroll deductions to fund certain employee benefits, such as insurance coverage for dependents.

R

(r) **Correlation Coefficient**
Measures the degree of correlation between two variables. The value range is between -1 and +1. A positive value shows a direct relationship; a negative value indicates an inverse relationship; a value

of 0 indicates that the two variables are independent; a value of 1 shows that the two variables are perfectly correlated.

(r2) **Coefficient of Determination**
Measures how good the estimated regression equation is—how good the fit is. The higher the r^2, the more confidence you should have on the estimated formula. A shortcut formula for r^2 used in a simple regression situation is:

$$r^2 = \frac{[n\Sigma xy - (\Sigma x)\,(\Sigma y)]^2}{[n\Sigma x^2 - (\Sigma x)^2]\,[n\Sigma x^2 - (\Sigma x)^2]}$$

R² **R-squared or standard deviation**
The percentage of a mutual fund's movement that can be explained by changes in the S&P. States that in 95 out of 100 cases, the fund's period-ending price will be plus or minus a certain percentage of the price at the beginning of the period.

RA **Restricted Account**
Margin account with a securities broker in which the equity is less than the initial margin set by Federal Reserve Board regulations.

RAM **Reverse Annuity Mortgage**
Mortgage loan that allows the homeowner-borrower (generally elderly) to live off of the substantial equity in the property.

RAR **Reserve/Asset Ratio**
Ratio of cash reserves to total tangible assets.

RB   **Revenue Bond**
                 See Municipal Revenue Bond.

RBFT   **Romanian Bank of Foreign Trade**

RC   **Registered Check**
                 Similar to a certified check, a check issued by a
                 bank for a customer who places funds aside in a
                 special account but does not have a regular check-
                 ing account.

RC   **Replacement Cost**
                 The cost to replace an asset or piece of property
                 with another of similar utility at current prices.

RCA   **Replacement Cost Accounting**
                 Practice of valuing assets and property at replace-
                 ment value.

R&D   **Research and Development**
                 Evolution of a new product or service, including
                 engineering, manufacturing and marketing.

RE   **Reversal of Prior Entry**
                 Accounting and bookkeeping notation that refers
                 to a journal or ledger entry that generally corrects
                 an entry previously made in error.

REDS   **Refunding Escrow Deposits**
                 Financial instruments that locks in a lower current
                 rate in anticipation of maturing higher-rate issues
                 by way of a forward purchase contract that oblig-
                 ates investors to buy bonds at a predetermined rate
                 when they are issued at a future date that coincides
                 with the first optional call date on existing high-
                 rate bonds. In the interim, investors' money is

invested in Treasury bonds, bought in the secondary market, which are held in escrow, effectively securing the investor's deposit and paying taxable annual income. The Treasuries mature around the call date on the existing bonds, thereby providing the money to buy the new issue and redeem the old one.

REIT **Real Estate Investment Trust**
Company, generally publicly traded, that invests shareholders' money in diversified real estate or mortgage portfolios rather than stocks. The three types of REITs are:

1. Equity REITs: Invest primarily in income-producing properties.
2. Mortgage REITs: Lend funds to developers or builders.
3. Hybrid REITs: Combination of equity and mortgage REITs.

REIT **Real Estate Investment Trust Fact Book**
(Fact Book) Annual publication published by the National Association of Real Estate Investment Trusts.

RELP **Real Estate Limited Partnership**
Limited partnership that invests in real estate and passes rental and other income through to limited partners.

REMIC **Real Estate Mortgage Investment Conduit**
Pass-through vehicle created in Tax Reform Act of 1986 for issuing multi-class mortgage-backed securities.

REO   **Real Estate Owned**
                        Real estate properties foreclosed upon or title
                        otherwise reverting to a lending institution.

RERC   **Real Estate Research Corporation**
                        Chicago-based organization that undertakes inde-
                        pendent research projects on trends and opportuni-
                        ties within the real estate industry.

RFP   **Request For Proposal**
                        Process by which a customer procures proposals
                        or bids for a service or product from one or more
                        prospective vendors, setting forth the customer's
                        specifications and expectations and asking that all
                        proposals follow certain guidelines so the
                        customer can make valid comparisons.

RHM   **RHM Survey of Warrants, Options &**
                        Low-Priced Stock
                        Weekly publication which provides investment
                        advice on warrants, call and put options and low-
                        priced stocks. Located in Glen Cove, NY.

RI   **Residual Income**
                        Operating income that an investment center can
                        earn above a minimum rate of return on
                        investment, expressed as an amount rather than a
                        percentage. Formula:

                        RI = Operating Income – (Minimum Required
                              Rate of Return x Operating Assets)

RIA   **Research Institute of America**
                        New York City-based publisher of a range of
                        widely used business reference materials.

RICO **Racketeer Influenced and Corrupt Organization Act**
Federal law used to prosecute firms and individuals of insider trading.

ROA **Return on Assets**
Ratio that shows whether management is using resources efficiently to produce a profit. If the ratio decreases over time, that shows that the productivity of assets in generating earnings has deteriorated.

Formula:
Return on Total Assets = $\dfrac{\text{Net Income}}{\text{Average Total Assets}}$

ROC **Return on Capital**
Distribution of cash resulting from depreciation tax savings, the sale of a capital asset or securities or any other transaction unrelated to retained earnings, also referred to as Return of Basis.

ROE **Return on Equity**
Earnings on a company's common stock investment for a given period, expressed as a percentage. The formula is:

ROE = $\dfrac{\text{Net income available to stockholders}}{\text{Average stockholders' equity}}$

ROI **Return on Investment**
Investments. General term for increased value of an amount invested over a stated period of time. The two key ratios are return on total assets and return on equity (ROE).

ROL   **Reduction Option Loan**
Hybrid between fixed-rate and adjustable rate
mortgage.

ROP   **Reorder Point**
Also called Economic Order Point, establishes
when to place a new order. Formula:

Reorder Point = Average usage per unit of lead
time x Lead time + Safety stock

Note: If average usage and lead time are both certain, then safety stock can be omitted from the
formula.

Example:
If lead time is 1 week, the year has 52 working
weeks and average usage per unit of lead time is
150 (7,800 pieces/52 weeks), the reorder point
150.

ROS   **Run on Schedule**
A product or service advertised on television or
radio when it's suitable for programming. Usually
means a lower rate.

ROS   **Return on Sales**
Net pretax profits as a percentage of net sales.

RP; REPO   **Repurchase Agreement**
Agreement between a buyer and seller of securities in which the seller agrees to repurchase the
securities at an agreed upon price, usually at a
stated time.

RP   **Reserve Purchase**
Indicates a purchase, generally of a capital asset,

being made from reserve funds as opposed to an operating budget.

RRM **Rate of Return Method**
General term to provide a category for a number of refined rate of return methods being used in analyzing investments.

RRM **Renegotiable Rate Mortgage or Renegotiated Rate Mortgage**
Mortgage loan in which the lender requires the borrower to renegotiate and requalify at specified intervals during the term of the loan.

RRP **Recommended Retail Price.**
Indicates a manufacturer's recommendation to retailers of pricing for a given item of merchandise.

RRR **Required Rate of Return**
Indicates the minimum return an investor will accept in order to participate or invest.

RRSP **Registered Retirement Savings Plan**
Tax-deductible and tax-sheltered retirement plan for Canadian taxpayers, similar to Individual Retirement Account (IRA) plans in the U.S.

RS **Revenue Sharing**
Return of tax revenue to one unit of government by a larger unit, such as from a state to one of its municipalities. Investments. percentage split between the general partner and limited partners of profits, losses, etc.

RTC   **Resolution Trust Corporation**
                   U.S. Government agency created in 1989 to merge
                   or close insolvent savings and loan institutions and
                   to liquidate their assets

RWA   **Returned without Action**
                   An export license in international trade that is sub-
                   mitted because there is a missing or incorrect item.
                   Once the correction is made, the application is
                   resubmitted.

S

S   **Savings; Expenditure Saved**
                   Indicates an amount reserved for investment or
                   budgeted for expenditure but not spent.

SA   **Savings Account**
                   Interest-earning deposit account at a commercial
                   bank, savings bank, or savings and loan
                   association.

SB   **Savings Bond**
                   U.S. government bond issued at a discount of their
                   face value and earning interest to and sometimes
                   beyond maturity, the interest being exempt from
                   state and l l taxes, and sometimes from federal
                   taxes.

S&D   **Special and Differential Treatment**
                   Special considerations given to the exports of
                   developing countries to improve their economic
                   and financial base. This may include lower or no
                   tariffs and the easing of trade barriers.

SAIF   **Savings Association Insurance Fund**
U.S. Government entity created in 1989 to replace
FSLIC as source of deposit insurance for thrift
institutions

S&L   **Savings and Loan Association**
Federally or state chartered depository financial
institution that obtains the bulk of its deposits from
consumers and holds the majority of its assets as
home mortgage loans.

S&L, S/L   **Sale and Leaseback or Sale-Leaseback**
Simultaneous purchase of real estate and lease
back to the seller, generally on a long-term lease.
The seller-lessee receives the proceeds of the sale
while retaining occupancy of the property.

SAM   **Shared Appreciation Mortgage**
Mortgage loan involving two co-borrowers, generally one of whom occupies the property. Less frequently called a SEM – Shared Equity Mortgage,
and informally called a CYD – "Call Your Dad"
mortgage.

SAMA   **Saudi Arabian Monetary Agency**

SAR   **Semi-Annual Report**
Any financial or management report produced or
published at the midpoint of the fiscal year.

SAS   **Statement on Auditing Standards**
Rule of auditing standards developed and issued
by the Financial Accounting Standards Board.

SB   **Statement of Billing**
Invoice for products or services sold.

SBC   **Swiss Bank Corporation**

SBA   **Small Business Administration**
U.S. Government agency providing management
and financial assistance to businesses that lack the
resources to pursue capital and other advantages
available to larger corporations. The SBA also has
a 24-hour electronic bulleting board that provides
information on SBA export and financial assistance, speakers, a women's mentor program,
minority programs, and a mailbox for electronic
discussions. The toll free numbers are: 1-800-859-
4646 (2400 baud modem); 1-800-697-4636 (9600
baud modem).

SBLA   **Small Business Loans Act**
Canadian legislation providing government funding for small business owners.

SBU   **Strategic Business Unit**
A unit within an organization that sells a distinct
set of products and services to an identified customer base in competition with well-defined com-
petitors. These units operate within the objectives
and strategies of top management.

SC   **Service Charge**
Designates an amount being billed to a customer
or an account for a specific service being
provided.

SCD   **Senior Citizen Discount**
Designates a price reduction (generally a percentage) for customers over a certain age (generally
65).

SCORE　　　　**Service Corps of Retired Executives**
National organization that matches retired executives offering their skills and experience with organizations that need short-term consulting and other services.

SD　　　　**Safe Deposit**
Bank service providing safekeeping for valuables, important documents, etc.

SD　　　　**Sight Draft**
Draft payable upon presentation by the designee.

SD　　　　**Standard Deduction**
An individual taxpayer's alternative to itemizing deductions on an income tax return.

SD　　　　**Stock Dividend**
Payment of a corporate dividend in the form of stock rather than cash.

SDFS　　　　**Same-Day Funds Settlement**
Method of settlement in good-the-same-day federal funds.

SDR　　　　**Special Drawing Rights**
Measure of a nation's reserve assets in the international monetary system.

S_e　　　　**Standard Error of the Estimate**
The standard deviation of the regression used to determine some concept of the accuracy of a prediction. The formula is:

$$S_{\hat{e}} = \sqrt{\frac{\sum (y - y')^2}{n - 2}} = \sqrt{\frac{\sum y^2}{}}$$

SE   **Self-Employed, Self-Employment**
Earning one's living directly from one's own profession or business, as opposed to as an employee earning salary, commissions or wages.

SE   **Shareholders Equity**
Total assets minus total liabilities: Net Worth.

SE   **Single-Entry Bookkeeping**
Simple accounting system noting only amounts owed by and due to a business.

SEC   **Securities and Exchange Commission**
U.S. Government agency that promotes full public disclosure and protects the investing public against malpractice in securities investments.

Location:
Securities and Exchange Commission
450 5th Street, N.W.
Washington, D.C. 20549

SEI   **Self-Employment Income**
Taxable income earned through self-employment as opposed or in addition to salary, wage and commission income from an employer.

SEM   **Shared-Equity Mortgage**
See SAM – Shared Appreciation Mortgage.

SEP   **Simplified Employee Pension**
Pension plan in which both the employee and employer contribute to the employee's Individual Retirement Account (IRA), with tax benefits and compliance requirements for both employee and employer.

SERP   **Self-Employed Retirement Plan**
Tax-deferred pension plan for self-employed individuals and employees of small, unincorporated businesses, also called Keogh Plan.

SES   **Stock Exchange of Singapore**

SET   **Securities Exchange of Thailand**

SF   **Sinking Fund**
Money accumulated on a regular basis in a separate custodial account that is used to extinguish an indebtedness, usually a bond issue.

SFAS   **Statement of Financial Accounting Standards**
Rule of accounting practice developed and issued by the Financial Accounting Standards Board (FASB).

SFSE   **San Francisco Stock Exchange**

SH   **Stockholder or Shareholder**
Individual or organization with an ownership position in a corporation

SI   **Simple Interest**
Calculation of interest based only on the original principal amount, rather than interest compounding over the term of the loan.

SIA   **Society of Industrial Accountants**
                 Canadian trade organization.

SIA   **Securities Industry Association**
                 U.S. trade group representing securities broker-
                 dealers.

SIC   **Standard Industrial Classification System**
                 Federally designed standard numbering system
                 identifying companies by industry and providing
                 other information.

SIMPLE   **Savings Incentive Match Plan for Employees**
                 Retirement plan created by the Taxpayer Relief
                 Act of 1997.

SIO   **Senior Information Officer**
                 Common job title.

SIPC   **Securities Investor Protection Corporation**
                 Nonprofit organization established by Congress
                 that insures securities and cash in customer
                 accounts of member brokerage firms

SIOR   **Society of Industrial and Office Realtors**
                 Washington, D.C.-based trade organization, affili-
                 ated with the National Association of Realtors.

S/M; S&M   **Service/Maintenance or Service and**
                 Maintenance
                 Designates an income or expense category for ser-
                 vice and maintenance of equipment, facilities, etc.

SML   **Security Market Line**
                 This line graph shows the relationship between

risk as measure by BET and the required rate of return for individual securities. The equation is:

Required rate of return = Risk-free rate + Stock's BETA x market risk premium

SNB **Swiss National Bank**

SO **Sales Order or Stock Order**
Documentation or record-keeping system, usually numbered serially, of orders placed and processed.

SOP **Standard of Practice**
One of a series of guidelines published by the AICPA to assist practitioners in adhering to high standards of ethics and consistency in completing engagements.

SOP **Standard Operating Procedure or Standard Operating Plan**
An organization's official statement of its routine or expected method for executing a specific task or responding to a certain situation.

S&P **Standard and Poor's**
Company that provides a broad range of investment services, primarily rating bonds and stocks, and compiling indexes and publishing statistics, advisory reports and financial information.

SP **Stop Payment**
Revocation of payment on a written check after the check has been sent or delivered to a payee.

SPA   **Societe per Azionie**

An Italian term for public corporation. The corporation must have at least two shareholders at formation.

SPDA   **Single-Premium Deferred Annuity**

Tax-deferred investment similar to an Individual Retirement Account but without many of an IRA's restrictions.

SPWL   **Single-Premium Whole Life (Insurance)**

Low-risk investment life insurance policy in which for a one-time payment of a minimum amount, the policyholder receives a paid-up insurance policy. The money is invested at a guaranteed rate of interest for one year or longer.

Features of SPWL:
1. The cash value earns interest at competitive rates from the date of the policy.
2. The policyholder can borrow interest earned annually after the first year.
3. The policyholder can take out a low-interest loan for 90% of the principal.
4. The policyholder receives permanent life insurance coverage.
5. Withdrawals and loans before age 59-1/2 are subject to a nondeductible tax penalty.
6. Cash value accumulates tax-deferred.
7. Death benefits are paid to beneficiaries tax-free.

Significant disadvantages:
1. Surrender charges are generally incurred if the money is taken out.
2. The interest rate is generally guaranteed for only one year, and can decrease.

SREA   **Senior Real Estate Analyst**
                   Professional certification offered by the Society of
                   Real Estate Appraisers

SRO   **Self-Regulatory Organization**
                   Any organization formed by various parties with-
                   in a trade or industry to provide governance and
                   oversight independent of government controls.

SRP   **Salary Reduction Plan**
                   Employee benefit program that allows employees
                   contribute compensation to qualified retirement or
                   other benefit plan on a pretax basis.

SS   **Social Security**
                   Aggregate taxpayer benefits under the Social
                   Security Act of 1935.

SSA   **Social Security Administration**
                   U.S. Government agency responsible for main-
                   taining and administering the Social Security
                   program.

ST   **Sales Tax**
                   State and/or local government tax based on a per-
                   centage of the selling price of goods and services.

STL   **Short-Term Loan**
                   Loan expected to be repaid within one year.

STAGS   **Sterling Transferable Accruing Government
                   Securities**
                   British bonds backed by British Treasury
                   securities.

S/V   **Surrender Value**
Amount of money an insurer will return to a policyholder upon cancellation of a policy.

SWIFT   **Society for Worldwide Interbank Financial Communications**
A worldwide dedicated computer network that provides funds transfer messages between member banks.

T

TA   **Tangible Asset**
Any asset other than a nonphysical right to something presumed to represent an advantage in the marketplace, such as goodwill, patents and trademarks.

T/A   **Trade Acceptance**
A time draft or date draft which is similar to a banker's acceptance. The difference is that a bank is not a party.

TAA   **Trade Adjustment Assistance**
The TAA is a United States policy authorized by the 1974 Trade Act to offer aid to workers laid off due to competition from imported goods. Such assistance includes job placement, instruction, and relocation support.

TAB   **Tax Anticipation Bill**
Short-term obligation issued by the U.S. Treasury.

TAC **Total Annualized Cost**
Projected expense in a given category over a 12-month period.

TAM **Tax Advisory Memoranda**
Significant statements of position and interpretation on the Internal Revenue Code that are issued as needed by Treasury Department.

TAN **Tax Anticipation Note**
Short-term obligation of a state or municipal government to finance current expenditures pending receipt of expected tax payments.

TAP **Total Annualized Profit**
Projected revenue less expense in a given category over a 12-month period.

T&B **Time and Billing (Software)**
Computer software that tracks hours incurred by activity for different staff for a particular client or project. Sources of time information include hourly rates, time sheets, practice management reports, and financial reports. At the end of each period, a bill is prepared based on hours worked and billing rates for each individual reporting time for each client and/or project.

TBE **Tenancy by the Entirety**
Individual co-ownership that passes automatically upon the death of one co-owner to the surviving co-owner.

T.C. **Tax Court**
U.S. federal tax court.

TD   **Time Draft**
                 Draft payable at a specified date in the future, as
                 opposed from a Sight Draft, which is payable upon
                 presentation.

TDAIR   **Taxpayer Delinquent Account Information
                 Record**
                 IRS recordkeeping mechanism.

TDI   **Taxpayer Delinquent Investigation**
                 IRS term for routine follow up on past-due tax
                 and/or penalty matters.

TE   **Total Expenditure**
                 Sum of all expenses in a given category.

T&E   **Travel and Entertainment**
                 Account for tracking and reimbursing travel and
                 entertainment expenses.

TEFRA   **Tax Equity and Fiscal Responsibility Act**
                 Federal legislation of 1982.

10-K   **Annual 10-K Report**
                 Contains the same the same type of information as
                 a company's annual report, but in greater detail. It
                 is the most widely known and can be obtained free
                 directly from the company or from the SEC for a
                 copying charge.

10-Q   **Quarterly 10-Q Report**
                 A report filed by a corporation when it experiences
                 an important event that stockholders would be
                 interested in knowing about. Such changes include
                 bankruptcy, change in control and officer or direc-
                 tor resignations.

THLRA   **Taft-Hartley Labor Relations Act**
Also known as Labor Management Relations Act, passed into law in 1947, provisions of which include injunctions against labor strikes.

TI   **Taxable Income**
Income or revenue subject to local, state or federal income tax.

TIC   **Tenancy in Common**
Ownership of real estate by two or more individuals, in which ownership at the death of one co-owner is part of the co-owner's disposable estate.

TIF   **Taxpayer Information File**
IRS term for recordkeeping mechanism.

TIGER   **Treasury Investors Growth Receipt**
U.S. government-backed bonds that are sold at deep discounts to investors, who receive no periodic investors but receive full face value at maturity.

TILA   **Truth in Lending Act**
Federal legislation enacted in 1968 that requires lenders to disclose to borrowers the true cost of loans and make interest rates and terms of loans simple to understand.

TIRA   **Thrift Industry Recovery Act**
Federal legislation enacted in 1987.

TL   **Total Loss**
Asset or property holding no present or future value because of damage, market reversal, etc.

TLI   **Term Life Insurance**
Life insurance policy written for a specific time period and paying the beneficiaries only in the event of the insured's death.

TMWR   **Tax Management Weekly Report**
Reference publication from Bureau of National Affairs (BNA).

TO   **Treasury Obligation**
Any negotiable U.S. Treasury debt obligation.

TP   **Taxpayer**
Any person who pays a tax or is subject to taxation.

TPR   **Temporary Price Reduction**
Short-term lowering of retail or whole sale price on a given product or service.

TPT   **Third-Party Transaction**
Business agreement executed through a bank or other third party.

TR   **Tax Rate**
Percentage of tax to be paid on a certain level of income.

TRA   **Tax Reform Act**
Major federal legislation enacting provisions affecting taxation.

TRSA   **Tax Reduction and Simplification Act**
Federal legislation enacted in 1977

TS   **Tax Shelter**

Mechanism used by an investor to legally avoid or reduce tax liabilities.

TS   **Treasury Stock**

Nonvoting stock created by a company to accomplish specific objectives and which does not pay or accrue dividends.

TSA   **Tax-Sheltered Annuity**

An employee-benefit plan similar to a 401(k) plan but available to employees of nonprofit organizations that are ineligible for a 401(k). With a TSA, an employee can withdraw funds at any age for any reason without tax penalty, and must pay ordinary taxes on all withdrawals.

TSOP   **Time Share Ownership Plan**

Mechanism in which multiple owners of a piece of real estate (*e.g.*, vacation home) purchase a specific block of time for use of the property each year.

TTA   **Total Tax Expenditures**

Sum of all taxes paid during a given accounting or financial reporting period.

12b-1   **12b-1 Plans**

Mutual fund fees that cover the cost of advertising and marketing. The main purpose of 12b-1 plans is to bring in new customers and, thus, more money for the fund to invest. The actual cost to the fund of a 12b-1 plan are listed in the front of the prospectus in the fee table.

U

UB   **Unemployment Benefits**
                 Payments made from federal and state unemploy-
                 ment insurance systems to laid-off workers, fund-
                 ed by a payroll tax on employers.

UBIT   **Unrelated Business Income Tax**
                 Tax on income to nonprofit organizations that is
                 unrelated to the purpose for which the organiza-
                 tion holds tax-exempt status.

UBTI   **Unrelated Business Taxable Income**
                 Income to a nonprofit organization that is taxable
                 as being unrelated to the reason for which the
                 organization holds tax-exempt status.

UCC   **Uniform Commercial Code**
                 Legal code adopted by most states that encom-
                 passes various laws dealing with commercial
                 transactions.

UGMA   **Uniform Gifts to Minors Act**
                 Federal legislation that provides for simple trans-
                 fer of assets to a minor without a formal trust or
                 guardianship.

UIT   **Unit Investment Trust**
                 Investment comprising portfolios of fixed-income
                 securities.

UOT   **Unit of Trading**
                 Normal number of shares, bonds or commodities
                 that make up the minimum unit of trading on an
                 exchange.

UN   **Unrealized Loss**
Loss that will not become actual until the security or property involved is sold, also called a paper loss.

UP   **Unrealized Profit**
Profit that will not become actual until the security or property involved is sold, also called a paper profit.

UPC   **Universal Product Code**
System for assigning a unique bar code to a product or type of property, read using special scanning equipment and used for inventory and other management purposes.

UPD   **Unpaid**
Indicates an amount due or invoice not paid in full.

UPT   **Undistributed Profits Tax**
Surtax on earnings retained in a business to avoid higher personal income taxes, also called Accumulated Profits Tax and Accumulated Earnings Tax.

USBS   **United States Bureau of Standards**
Federal government agency.

USCC   **United States Chamber of Commerce**
Federal government agency.

USIT   **Unit Share Investment Trust**
Special type of Unit Investment Trust.

USLSI   **United States League of Savings Institutions**
National trade organization.

V

V/A   **Value Added**
Concept of building additional benefits into a
product or service to make it more attractive to
prospective customers and to retain existing
customers.

VAT   **Value Added Tax**
In the European Common Market, consumption
tax charged at stages of manufacturing and at time
of purchase.

VC   **Venture Capital**
Source of financing for start-up companies and
businesses undertaking major new developments.

VELDA SUE   **Venture Enhancement and Loan
Development Administration for Smaller
Undercapitalized Enterprises**
U.S. Government agency

VFD   **Value for Duty**
Worth of goods on which tariff for importation,
exportation or consumption is charged.

VIR   **Variable Interest Rate**
Interest rate that rises or falls based on changes in
interest rates in an index of interest rates.

VLI   **Variable Life Insurance**
Insurance policy in which the cash value of the
policy is invested in stock, bond or money market
portfolios.

VPA   **Volume Purchase Agreement**
Contract for purchasing a large quantity of a given
product, generally at a significant discount based
on the quantity.

VRM   **Variable Rate Mortgage**
Similar to ARM (Adjustable Rate Mortgage),
which is more often used.

VSE   **Vienna Stock Exchange**

W

WACC   **Weighted Average Cost of Capital**
Rate of return an investor could expect in another
investment with equivalent risk, also called
Opportunity Cost.

WAN   **Wide Area Network**
A computer network comprising a large geograph-
ic area.

WATS   **Wide Area Telephone Service**
Lower-rate long distance telephone lines used by
businesses.

WC   **Working Capital**
Current assets minus current liabilities.

WCRI   **Workers Compensation Research Institute**
Cambridge, Mass.-based organization providing
research and other information resources on workers compensation insurance rates and rules.

WDV   **Written Down Value**
                   Downward adjustment of the value of an asset
                   according to Generally Accepted Accounting
                   Principles (GAAP).

WH   **Withholding**
                   Deduction from salary or other compensation or
                   distributions for tax liabilities.

WH   **Work Hour(s)**
                   Unit of timekeeping as tracked for billing or pay-
                   ing wages for work provided.

wi   **When, as, and if issued**
                   Indicates that, if a stock is trading before it has
                   cleared all legal requirements for issuance, all
                   trades will be cancelled should the stock not be
                   issued.

W/O   **Write-Off**
                   To permanently charge an asset to expense or loss
                   as a means of resolving an uncollectable or irre-
                   trievably depreciated item.

WPT   **Windfall Profit Tax**
                   Tax on profits resulting from a sudden event favor-
                   able to a particular company or industry.

Ww   **With warrants**
                   Indicates that new issues of stock appear in units
                   that include a number of warrants that may be
                   detached and traded separately or remain with the
                   stock certificates as specified. A warrant is an
                   option that gives its holder the right to buy a secu-
                   rity at a set price, either within a specified period
                   of time or perpetually.

Y

YTD   **Year-to-Date**
Indicates that financial or other information shown reflects all occurrences in the current fiscal year through the present date.

YS   **Yield Spread**
The difference between the yields received on two different types of bonds with different ratings.

YTM   **Yield to Maturity**
Fully compounded rate of return on a bond, assuming the bond is held to maturity. The formula for estimating YTM on a bond issued at a discount is:

$$\frac{\text{Stated Amount of Interest} + \frac{\text{Discount}}{\text{Years to Maturity}}}{\frac{\text{Current Price of Bond} + \text{Maturity Value}}{2}}$$

The formula for computing an estimate of the YTM when a bond is issues at a premium is:

$$\frac{\text{Stated Amount of Interest} - \frac{\text{Premium}}{\text{Years to Maturity}}}{\frac{\text{Current Price of Bond} + \text{Maturity Value}}{2}}$$

Z

ZBB **Zero-Based Budgeting**
Method of developing budgets that requires
re-examination of all assumptions for both revenue and expenses, rather than adjustments to
prior years' budgets or actual results. The basic
steps are:

1. Determine objectives and activities required.
2. Evaluate alternative ways of accomplishing
   each activity.
3. Develop and review alternative budget figures
   for various possible future occurrences.
4. Formulate measurements for performance.
5. Rank activities in order of their importance to
   the organization.

ZSE **Zurich Stock Exchange**

Appendix I
Monetary Units

Country, Island or Territory	Currency	Symbol
Afghanistan	afghani	Af
Albania	lek	s
Algeria	dinar	DA
American Samoa	dollar	$
Angola	kwanza	Kz
Anguilla	dollar	EC$
Antarctica	krone	NKr
Argentina	peso	double-dashed
Australia	dollar	A$
Austria	schilling	S
Bahamas	dollar	B$
Bahrain	dinar	BD
Bangladesh	taka	Tk
Barbados	dollar	BdS$
Belgium	franc	BF
Belize	dollar	BZ$
Benin	franc	CFAF
Bhutan	ngultrum	Nu
Bolivia	peso	$b
Botswana	pula	P
Bouvet Island	krone	NKr
Brazil	Real	
British Indian Ocean Territory	rupee	Mau Rs
British Virgin Islands	dollar or pound	$ or £
Brunei	ringitt	B$

Country, Island or Territory	Currency	Symbol
Bulgaria	lev	Lv
Burkina Faso	franc	CFAF
Burundi	franc	FBu
Cameroon	franc	CFAF
Canada	dollar	Can$
Canton and Enderbury Islands	dollar	$
Cape Verde Island	escudo	C.V.Esc.
Central African Republic	franc	CFAF
Chad	franc	CFAF
Chile	peso	Ch$
China	yuan	Y
Christmas Island	dollar	A$
Cocos (Keeling) Islands	dollar	A$
Cook Islands	dollar	NZ$
Colombia	peso	Col$
Comoros	franc	CF
Congo	franc	CFAF
Costa Rica	colon	slashed C
Cyprus	pound	£C
Czech Republic	koruna	CK
Denmark	krone	Dkr
Djibouti	franc	DF
Dominica	dollar	EC$
Dominican Republic	peso	RD$
Dronning Maud Land	krone	NKr
Ecuador	sucre	S/
Egypt	pound	£E
El Salvador	colon	¢
Equatorial Guinea	ekwele	
Ethiopia	biria	Br
European Union	European Currency Unit	ecu
Faro Islands	krone	Dkr
Falkland Islands	pound	£F
Fiji	dollar	F$
Finland	markka	Fmk
France	franc	F
French Guiana	franc	F
French Polynesia	franc	CFPF
Gabon	franc	CFAF
Gambia	dalasi	D

Country, Island or Territory	Currency	Symbol
Germany	deutsche mark	DM
Ghana	cedi	¢
Gilbraltar	pound	£
Greece	drachma	Dr
Greenland	krone	Dkr
Grenada	dollar	EC$
Guadeloupe	franc	F
Guam	dollar	$
Guatemala	quetzal	Q
Guinea-Bissau	peso	PG
Guinea	syli	
Guyana	dollar	G$
Haiti	gourde	G
Heard and McDonald Islands	dollar	A$
Honduras	lempira	L
Hong Kong	dollar	HK$
Hungary	forint	Ft
Iceland	krÛna	IKr
India	rupee	Rs
Indonesia	rupiah	Rp
Iran	rial	Rls
Iraq	dinar	ID
Ireland	pound or punt	£ir
Israel	new shekel	IS
Italy	lira	Lit
Ivory Coast	franc	CFAF
Jamaica	dollar	J$
Japan	yen	¥
Johnston Island	dollar	$
Jordan	dinar	JD
Kampuchea	riel	CR
Kenya	shilling	K Sh
Kiribati	dollar	A$
Korea, North	won	Wn
Korea, South	won	W
Kuwait	dinar	KD
Laos	kip	KN
Latvia	Lats	Ls
Lesotho	loti, pl., maloti	L, pl., M
Liberia	dollar	$

Country, Island or Territory	Currency	Symbol
Libya	dinar	LD
Liechtenstein	franc	SwF
Luxembourg	franc	LuxF
Macao	pataca	P
Madagascar	franc	FMG
Malawi	kwacha	MK
Malaysia	ringgit	RM
Maldives	rufiyaa	Rf
Mali	franc	CFAF
Malta	lira	£m
Martinique	franc	F
Mauritania	ouguiya	UM
Mauritius	rupee	Mau Rs
Midway Islands	dollar	$
Mexico	peso	Mex$
Monaco	franc	F
Mongolia	tugrik	Tug
Montserrat	dollar	EC$
Morocco	dirham	DH
Mozambique	metical	Mt
Myanmar	kyat	K
Nauru	dollar	A$
Namibia	rand	R
Nepal	rupee	NRs
New Caledonia	franc	F
Netherlands	guilder	f.
Netherlands Antilles	guilder	Ant.f.
New Zealand	dollar	NZ$
Nicaragua	cordoba	C$
Niger	franc	CFAF
Nigeria	naira	N
Niue	dollar	NZ$
Norfolk Island	dollar	A$
Norway	krone	NKr
Oman	rial	RO
Pakistan	rupee	PRs
Panama	balboa	B
Panama Canal Zone	dollar	$
Papua New Guinea	kina	K
Paraguay	guarani	slashed G

Country, Island or Territory	Currency	Symbol
Peru	inti	I/
Philippines	peso	P
Pitcairns Islands	dollar	NZ$
Poland	zloty	Z dashed l
Portugal	escudo	Esc
Puerto Rico	dollar	$
Qatar	riyal	QR
Reunion	franc	F
Romania	franc	RF
San Marino	lira	Lit
Saudi Arabia	franc	CFAF
Seychelles	rupee	SR
Sierra Leone	leone	Le
Singapore	dollar	S$
Slovakia	koruna	Sk
Solomon Island	dollar	Sl$
Somalia	shilling	So. Sh.
South Africa	rand	R
Spain	peseta	Ptas
Sri Lanka	rupee	SLRs
St. Kitts and Nevis	dollar	EC$
St. Lucia	dollar	EC$
St. Vincent and Grenada	dollar	EC$
Sudan	pound	LSd
Suriname	krone	NKr
Swaziland	ilangeni, emalangeni	pl., L, Pl., E
Sweden	krona	Sk
Switzerland	franc	SwF
Syria	pound	LS
Taiwan	dollar	T$
Tanzania	shilling	TSh
Thailand	baht	Bht or Bt
Togo	franc	CFAF
Tokelau	dollar	NZ$
Tonga	pa'anga	PT
Trinidad and Tobago	dollar	TT$
Tunisia	dinar	D
Turkey	lira	LT
Turks and Caicos Islands	dollar	$

Country, Island or Territory	Currency	Symbol
Tuvalu	dollar	A$
Uganda	shilling	USh
United Arab Emeriates	dirham	Dh
United Kingdom	pound	£
United States of America	dollar	$
Uruguay	new peso	NUr$
Vanuatu	vatu	VT
Vatican	lira	Lit
Venezuela	bolivar	Bs
Viet Nam	dong	D
Virgin Islands	dollar	$
Wake Island	dollar	$
Wallis and Futuna Islands	franc	CFPF
Western Sahara	peseta	Ptas
Western Samoa	tala	WS$
Yemen	rial	YRls
Yugoslavia	dinar	Din
Zaire	zaire	Z
Zambia	kwacha	K
Zimbabwe	dollar	Z$

Appendix II
Major Sources

Barron's Dictionary of Finance and Investment Terms, Fourth ed., John Downes and Jordan Elliot Goodman, Barron's Educational Series, Inc., 1995.

Dictionary of Business Acronyms, Jennifer Mossman, Editor, Wynwood Press Edition published by special arrangement with Gale Research, Inc., 1991

Encyclopedia of Associations, 25th ed., Gale Research, Inc., 1996.

Investment Math Made Easy, Martin J. Miles, Prentice Hall, 1986.

Keys to Understanding the Financial News, Nick Apostolou, D.B.A., and D. Lawrence Crumbley, Ph.D., Barron's Business Keys, 1989.

Real Estate Financial Management, Second ed., David B. Doeleman, CRB, CRS, and Ronald C. Rogers, Ph.D., Realtors National Marketing Institute of the National Association of Realtors, 1986.

Word Smart, Executive Edition: Words for Suits, Liz Buffa, Random House, 1995.